Beyond Buffalo!

A Photographic Journey and Guide to the Secret Natural Wonders Of Our Region

David Lawrence Reade

Beyond Buffalo!

Outdoor activities are by their very nature potentially hazardous. All participants in such activities must assume the responsibility for their own actions and safety. The author and publisher assume no responsibility or liability for actions or occurrences should the reader choose to visit the places described in this book.

While all reasonable efforts were made to verify the accuracy of the material contained in this book, the author and publisher assume no responsibility or liability for errors, inaccuracies, or omissions.

Printed in Kenmore, New York by Partners' Press Inc.

ISBN 1-879201-19-4

Publisher:
Buffalo and Beyond
P.O. Box 326
Boston, New York 14025

Acknowledgments

In the past, while following a lifelong passion of seeking out and exploring new places, I would occasionally bring my camera along and record what I saw. Several friends were intrigued enough by my photographs to encourage me to think seriously about considering the possibility of making photography my life's work.

Since then, this book has been a dream of mine. Now it is no longer a dream, but a reality. ***Beyond Buffalo!*** never would have been possible without the help and encouragement of all the wonderful people I am proud to call family and friends. While it would be impossible to thank everyone who has influenced this book, I especially want to thank the following people (in alphabetical order):

Carol Aldrich - for her insights, encouragement and unwavering belief in my abilities.

Donna Felger - for book layout and design and for not letting near exhaustion affect the quality of her work during the final push.

Clarissa Harison - for encouraging me ever since first seeing my photographs to pursue photography as my life's work.

Tony Hitchcock and Jean Lindgren - for sharing with me the benefits of their experience, for encouraging me to follow my dreams and for providing me with opportunities to work with them while I was figuring out how.

Larry and Barbara Reade - for instilling in me a passion for things wild and natural and for helping me to see the book as others would see it.

Ken Wedlake - for spending many hours assisting me in the tedious color refinement process necessary for the printing of photographs in a book and for sharing with me his insights and enthusiasm about the book and photography in general.

Tracy Wedlake - for letting me steal her husband away so often and for a stellar job of proofreading.

Adrian Zannin - for all the times he dropped everything to assist me with my temperamental computer and for his insights, suggestions and unflagging support in all regards.

Also - Cheryl Campbell, Amy Caterina and the Campos Crew, Mike and Debbie Hahin, Dave and Sharon D'Ingillo, Mike Reade, Ron Reade, and George and Jane Rak of Hamburg Color Lab.

A special acknowledgement goes to the Campos Group for their contribution to the delicate process of ensuring that the vibrancy and spirit of the original scene was retained from the click of the shutter to the final printing of the image on the pages of this book. The state-of-the-art facilities and the knowledgeable and ever helpful staff of the Campos Group made this possible. They can be reached at 837-1016.

Introduction

This book is about pride. Pride in the area where we live, work and play. About building the esteem of our area. As a lifelong Western New Yorker, I'm frustrated with the myopic view of our region held by the national press. Together, let's journey beyond the Buffalo of public perception.

When people who have never been to this area are asked for their impressions of Buffalo, most often mentioned are snow, chicken wings, the professional sports teams and Niagara Falls. No doubt, these things are an important part of the character of our area. But, if you believe there is much more to our area than that of the national perception, join me on a fascinating journey to spectacular, yet little known places of natural beauty and interest in Western New York and the surrounding areas - guaranteed to give you a whole new appreciation of how truly special our region really is.

These are my own personal favorite destinations for an hour, a day or a weekend. These memorable sites are generally off the beaten path - a few you may have heard of but many you won't have. My purpose here is to expand your appreciation for the area and capture some of the true spirit of our little corner of the earth - by revealing some truly interesting places you may not have known existed, but that can rival other parts of the country for scenic beauty and interest.

This visual and literary celebration of our area is assembled in 'Coffeetable Book' style so that anyone can experience the splendor I have seen through my lens and through my prose. For those who would like to explore these places themselves, a full page reference map keyed to the Table of Contents is included, and each individual section features the 'QuikFinder™' locator tool along with complete directions.

This book is for anyone who takes pride in our area. For residents and business people alike, this book is a must for those of us who are proud to call this area home.

Book Organization

The featured places in this book are grouped into three categories based on distance from downtown Buffalo:

Anytimers - closest to (or in) the City of Buffalo, perfect for quick visits when you don't have a lot of time. Several are located in the city or the closest suburbs, the farthest are just over an hour away.

Daytrippers - great for when you have the whole day to explore. From about one and a half hours up to three hours drive time.

Weekenders - wonderful areas in which to spend the weekend. Anywhere from three and a half to six hours drive (and absolutely worth it!).

Beyond Buffalo!

Of course, if you decide to visit these places, you may spend more time than my category names imply (*in fact, these areas are so fascinating, you may want to plan on it*). A number of the locations are close to each other or along the way, so you may want to consider visiting several of them on the same trip.

The organization of the individual sections is as follows:

QuikFinder™. Located in the upper right hand corner on the first page of each section you will find the QuikFinder™ box. This box contains the following information: a mini-map showing the general vicinity of the place relative to Buffalo, the approximate driving mileage, direction and drivetime from Buffalo and the nearest town or city of consequence.

General Description. An overall description of the highlights and features of the area. The descriptions and impressions throughout this book are limited to my own personal knowledge. I do not claim to be an expert in any of the various disciplines of the natural sciences, however I have tried to the best of my ability to capture the overall feel of each of these places.

First Impressions. A recounting of how the 'spirit' of the place moved me during my first ever visit.

Special Spot Vignette. Every beautiful area has its 'special spot'. You know: the spot at the base of the waterfalls where at the right angle you can catch a shimmering rainbow hovering in the mist over the falling water or the apple orchard where you can be sure to spot feeding deer just before dusk. Or where, arriving just before sunrise, the only sounds you hear are the beautiful lilting melodies of songbirds resonating in dawn's early light.

Activities. A list of activities befitting the area. For more information on permissible activities contact the nearest local authorities (*see More Information* later in this *Introduction* section).

Amenities. For the **Anytimers** group, this section lists facilities on premises such as picnic shelters, restrooms, etc. In the **Daytrippers** and **Weekenders** groups, this section also indicates whether there are accommodations nearby.

Directions. For those of you who decide to visit, complete directions are provided from downtown Buffalo. If you are coming from another area, adapt the directions for your use by consulting local area road maps. All of the directions start on major highways that are easily accessed. While a significant effort was made to ensure that all the directions are accurate, I strongly recommend bringing local area road maps with you on your trip.

Why This Book and Why These Places?

Growing up in Western New York, I have heard all the disparaging remarks about the area. It's too cold. There's too much snow. There are two seasons - winter and the day before winter. There's nothing to do. There's no reason to stay here. The economy is terrible. Well, don't believe any of it. This area has too much to offer.

It is my contention that, while Western New York has been struggling economically of late and the winters can sometimes be frustrating, we are very fortunate to have such an assortment of everything here. Think about it, how many other places do you truly get such a wide cross section of natural attributes?

We have plenty of snow for winter sports. The summers are kept tolerable by the Great Lake air conditioners - Erie and Ontario. Did you know that Buffalo is the sunniest, driest city in the whole Northeast from May to September? And that the average number of snowfalls in Buffalo of over six inches is only two per winter? The majority of snow falls in just the right place - in the ski country in the hills to the south of the City.

Scenic hills, streams and forests abound in the area. The incredible Adirondack and Catskill Forever Wild Forest Preserves are within a half a days drive. If you want major big city excitement without having to live it, Toronto is just an hour and a half away.

We have some spectacular scenic treasures right in our own backyards that go wholly unappreciated - because most people don't even know they exist! I propose that we get out there and start appreciating what we have and stop focusing on the negative. An area with pride in itself will make things happen. And, if I can contribute to that pride - well, then I'm accomplishing what I set out to do!

The places featured in this book are special to me and I hope you will feel the same way about them whether you visit these places yourself or you only experience them vicariously through lens and pen. I've been exploring this area for years and believe that you will find these places worthy of the awe in which I hold them.

Each locale selected has its own special elements of beauty and many have a 'believe or not' aspect. You may find yourself saying things like "I wouldn't have believed that these boulders were bigger than my house if I weren't seeing them for myself" or "these fantastic rock shapes look like they belong in Utah or Arizona". In short, each of these locales has touched me in its own unique way.

Beyond Buffalo!

The selection criteria used varies - for instance, Glen Falls in Williamsville is surely not the most spectacular place included in this book, but it is close to Buffalo and an exceptional little park with a beautiful waterfall. It is a great escape from the incessant traffic of Main Street less than a couple hundred yards away - a real treasure for those who visit this park.

Another objective in the selection process was to avoid extremely well known places of which there is already plenty written and of which many good photographs abound. An obvious example is Niagara Falls. Almost everyone in this area has been there and certainly there are many good books available about the Falls. I have found delight in discovering intriguing places that are off the beaten path - places that many of you have never visited (and in some cases, may never have even heard of!).

Some of the selections are New York State Parks. The majority of the State Parks included in this book, like Buttermilk Falls, Taughannock Falls, Whetstone Gulf and Chimney Bluffs are unknown to the average Buffalonian. When conducting an informal, random poll, I found few people who were aware of any of these four spectacular parks.

State Parks usually have truly standout features that motivated someone with foresight to decide that it should be preserved for all of us to enjoy. Buttermilk Falls contains a half-mile long trail of non-stop waterfalls, cascades and incredible rock sculptures. Taughannock has the highest straight drop waterfalls in the entire Northeastern United States, higher than the mighty Niagara! Whetstone Gulf is an impressive canyon carved straight down into the indominitable Tug Hill Plateau. Chimney Bluffs is like visiting a whole different world reminiscent of the rock sculptures of the Southwest. Allegany is so extensive that even though many of you have been there, you may have missed some important features. Evangola has the largest (and most interesting) public beach on Lake Erie anywhere near Buffalo. And surprisingly, many people have never visited 'The Eighth Wonder of the World' - Watkins Glen!

In my opinion, the State has done an excellent job balancing two opposing forces: volumes of people vs. nature. In most of the State Parks featured in *Beyond Buffalo!*, the structural elements are constructed to blend well with the surrounding environment and the areas off the beaten path have been left as natural as possible.

Many of the places included in this book can be visited in a series. For example, I would recommend visiting Buttermilk Falls of Leroy and Chimney Bluffs on the same day. Or take a long weekend to visit Inman Gulf, Whetstone Gulf and the Stillwater/ Beaver River area. Take a day (or two) to visit the featured areas of Zoar Valley and the Deer Lick Nature Preserve together. Another trip meriting a weekend would be the Finger Lakes region, making it part of your itinerary to visit Watkins Glen, Taughannock Falls and Buttermilk Falls.

On the other hand, the Killarney Wilderness Park in Canada and the Pine Creek area (Pennsylvania's Grand Canyon) are extensive and beg to be visited exclusively for several days to be fully appreciated.

Once you visit some of these places you may feel new pride for our area. Sometimes knowledge is power - that is, when we gain new insight into how special our region really is, we will start to tell the whole world.

Volume II?

I have gathered a substantial amount of information toward a second volume through my own on-going explorations and through others who have alerted me to places that I had not been previously aware of.

Share your personal secret place. If the area is open to the public, I would like to consider including it in Volume II.

Contacting the author:

David Lawrence Reade
c/o Buffalo and Beyond
Post Office Box 326
Boston, New York 14025

E-mail: dlreade@buffalo-and-beyond.com

. . . the enjoyment of scenery employs the mind without fatigue and yet exercises it; tranquillizes it and yet enlivens it; and thus, through the influence of the mind over the body, gives the effect of refreshing rest and reinvigoration to the whole system.

- Frederick Law Olmsted

More Information

*In **New York***, contact:

The Department of Environmental Conservation
270 Michigan Avenue
Buffalo, NY 14203
716-851-7000
- or -
Travel & Tourism
1-800-225-5697
www.iloveny.state.ny.us

For places in **Ontario**, call:

Ontario Travel Information
1-800-668-2746
www.travelinx.com
- or -
Natural Resources Information Centre
416-314-2000

For **Pennsylvania** information contact:

Bureau of State Parks
P.O. Box 1467
Harrisburg, PA 17105-1467
1-800-63-PARKS
www.parec.com/penn
- or -
The U.S. Forest Service
222 Liberty St.
P.O. Box 847
Warren, PA 16365
1-814-723-5150

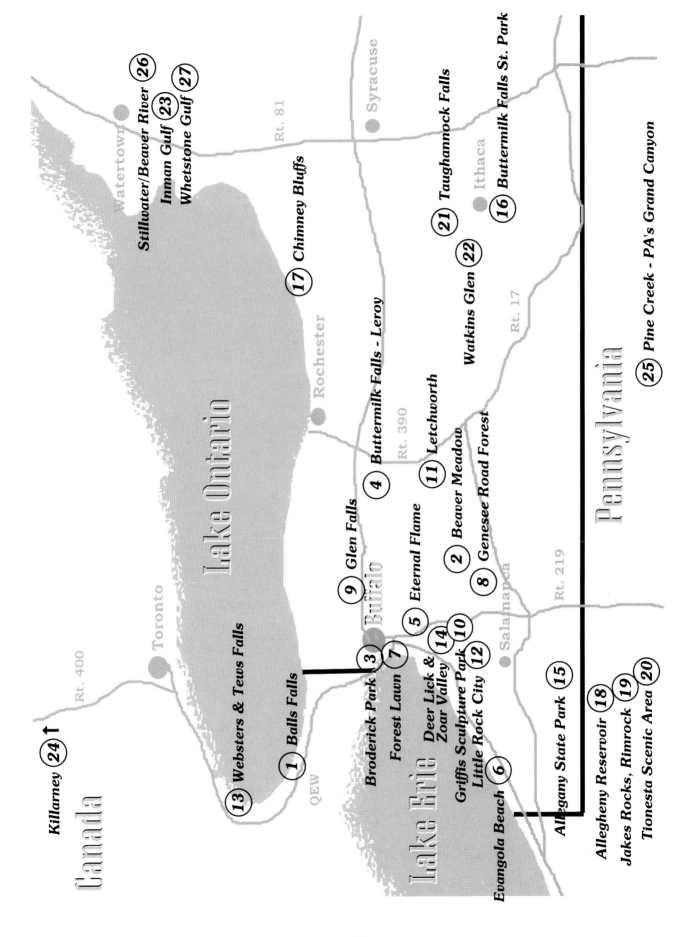

Canada

Killarney ㉔ ↑

Lake Ontario

Lake Erie

Toronto

Rt. 400

QEW

Buffalo

Watertown

Rt. 81

Syracuse

Ithaca

Rochester

Salamanca

Rt. 390

Rt. 17

Rt. 219

Pennsylvania

① Balls Falls
② Beaver Meadow
③ Broderick Park
④ Buttermilk Falls - Leroy
⑤ Eternal Flame
⑥ Evangola Beach
⑦ Forest Lawn
⑧ Genesee Road Forest
⑨ Glen Falls
⑩ Deer Lick & Zoar Valley
⑪ Letchworth
⑫ Little Rock City
⑬ Websters & Tews Falls
⑭ Griffis Sculpture Park
⑮ Allegany State Park
⑯ Buttermilk Falls St. Park
⑰ Chimney Bluffs
⑱ Allegheny Reservoir
⑲ Jakes Rocks, Rimrock
⑳ Tionesta Scenic Area
㉑ Taughannock Falls
㉒ Watkins Glen
㉓ Inman Gulf
㉔ Killarney
㉕ Pine Creek - PA's Grand Canyon
㉖ Stillwater/Beaver River
㉗ Whetstone Gulf

CONTENTS

CONTENTS

Anytimers

Balls Falls Conservation Area

Upper and Lower Balls Falls were created by Twenty Mile Creek tumbling over the Niagara Escarpment. The Niagara Escarpment is a long bluff of exceedingly hard limestone which was once the shoreline of ancient Lake Ontario. It stretches from Western New York deep into the province of Ontario. Many falls tumble over the escarpment among which Niagara Falls is the most famous.

QuikFinder™

Distance	45 miles
Direction	NW
Nearest City/Town	St. Catherines
Drivetime	1 hour

Both Lower and Upper Balls Falls are impressive. The drop of the lower falls is nearly 100 feet and the water has cut an almost perfect semi-circle through the picturesque layers of rock. The upper falls are shorter in stature but just as fascinating in structure. There are gentle, paved footpaths to the top of both falls making the views accessible to almost anyone. Viewing either falls from below requires rock scrambling and moderate hiking skills.

Water coursing over the brink of Upper Balls Falls in late autumn.

Beyond Buffalo!

First Impression

It was a cool, sunny early spring day. Snow, the last vestige of winter, was melting everywhere. The stream running through the park was brimming but gave no hint of the incredible waterfalls that lie just out of sight and earshot.

Not knowing there were two sets of falls, I followed the only path I saw upstream and found the upper falls. As I scrambled down into the valley below for a better view, I was soaked almost instantly by huge clouds of mist lifted into the air by the great volumes of water crashing over the brink.

Cold and wet but satisfied, I returned to the parking lot prepared to leave. Just then another path caught my eye. I followed it to the top of the lower falls and saw torrents of water arcing out from a rock ledge, then plummeting nearly 100 feet into the gorge below. And to top things off, a beautiful glistening rainbow was suspended in mid-air across the gorge!

Special Spot

Contemplating the awe inspiring force of falling water from the base of the lower falls. From this vantage point there are few reminders of civilization, just some of the ever-present forces of nature - wind, mist and thundering water.

Activities

Balls Falls Conservation Area offers all the typical activity opportunities of a day use park - picnicking, hiking, nature appreciation, photography, ball playing, roller blading and cross-country skiing and snowshoeing in the winter. It also offers a bit of history reenacted in the form of a rebuilt pioneer cabin with a stockade area and barn that are available for tour.

Amenities

The park has picnic shelters, benches, grills and public restrooms. There is a charge for parking.

Directions

From downtown Buffalo, enter the Niagara Section of the NYS Thruway (Route 190) headed north. Follow the signs to the Peace Bridge and enter Canada. As you proceed from the customs area, take the Queen Elizabeth Way west. After approximately 35 miles and after passing several St. Catharines exits, look for the sign directing you to the Balls Falls Conservation Area. Exit here (exit 57) to Route 24 and turn left (on Route 24). Proceed about 3.7 miles until you see the Conservation Area sign. Turn left onto Regional Road 75. After the one lane bridge over Twenty Mile Creek you will see the parking area on your right.

Beaver Meadow Audubon Center

QuikFinder™

Distance	30 miles
Direction	ESE
Nearest City/Town	Java Village
Drivetime	45 minutes

Beaver Meadow is a 324-acre nature sanctuary featuring 5.5 miles of trails, a visitor center, an astronomical observatory, walkways for the blind and handicapped, observations decks, a sugar shanty, an amphitheater, trailside exhibits and much more.

The purpose of Beaver Meadow is "to inspire a wider appreciation and understanding of nature". Beaver Meadow is sponsored by the Buffalo Audubon Society, Inc., as a not-for-profit educational center. There are many educational programs offered for both children and adults. The Center is comprised as a sanctuary where all living things are safe from human destruction.

Beaver Meadow is not supported by state or federal funds. If you wish to find out about becoming a member of the Buffalo Audubon Society or becoming a Beaver Meadow Booster, call 716-457-3228 or write to:

Beaver Meadow Audubon Center
1610 Welch Road
North Java, New York 14113

First Impression

Hiking around Beaver Meadow on the beautifully maintained trails and fraternizing with myriad waterfowl and animals living in and around the ponds and forest made me feel infinitely more connected to nature and the beauty of our world.

Special Spot

Arrive before sunrise on a cool, clear day. Quietly walk the lake trail where you will see and hear the ducks, geese and songbirds preparing for the day ahead. Chances are you will have the trail to yourself, especially on a weekday. I understand that most people just don't want to get up that early, but trust me, at Beaver Meadow it is well worth missing a little extra sleep or going to bed a little bit earlier!

Activities

The list goes on forever: guided tours for school groups, scouts, adult groups, church associations and garden clubs; family programs; night walks; owl prowls; a nature festival; summer day camp; bird and butterfly counts; hiking; photography; nature appreciation and, by winter, snowshoeing and cross-country skiing (with rentals available). In deference to the wildlife, a few things that are not allowed are: fires, pets, off-trail wandering, smoking, littering, collecting or any activity which will disturb the wildlife or environment.

The first sun illuminates the early morning quiet of Beaver Meadow

There are dozens of named, well maintained trails. You can pick up a trail map at the visitor center.

One of my favorite trails is the Old Homestead Trail, a self-guided trail using a pamphlet from the visitor center. The trail takes you through some of the human history of the area. What at first looks to the untrained eye like just meadows, ponds and woods, comes alive as you read about the history of the area. You can picture the people who lived on this land as you see old foundations, barb wire fencing imbedded deep in the trees and a tine from a horse drawn hay rake buried in the V of a tree. There is also a sugar house to visit along the way where maple sugar and syrup are made.

'Two headed' ducks reflect the serenity of the Beaver Pond.

For those of you who love nature, enjoy being around people and feel like you would like to give something back, Beaver Meadow is always looking for volunteers for a variety of activities. I relish the spring I had the opportunity to give tours of the center to school children several times a week. To inquire about volunteering, contact Beaver Meadow at the telephone number given previously.

Amenities

The visitor center features a 'hands on' discovery room where you can see what a beaver skull looks like or feel a raccoon pelt. The center also has live animals including snakes and turtles. Other features of the center include the gift shop (where the proceeds go directly towards supporting the center), observation windows and deck overlooking the main pond and bird feeders, a weather station, a library and meeting rooms.

Also on the grounds is an astronomical observatory. The observatory houses one of the most powerful telescopes in Western New York. It is open at scheduled times and when special events are taking place in the night skies - call the center for more information.

For the blind or handicapped, the Jenny Glen wooden walkway provides a way for everyone to appreciate Beaver Meadow. The walkway, which is elevated just above the marsh, features handrails on both sides and strategically placed wood benches for resting and immersing oneself in nature.

Directions

From downtown Buffalo, access the Niagara section of the NYS Thruway (Route 190) heading south. After about five miles pick up the mainline NYS Thruway (Route 90) heading west. Stay to your right and exit to Route 400 South. After about eleven miles, exit at Route 20A & 78 headed east (away from the village of East Aurora). After two miles, follow Route 78 where it branches off from 20A heading south. After approximately eight miles on Route 78 you will enter the village of Java. Turn left onto Welch Road and follow it two miles to Route 77. Continue straight on Welch Rd. across Route 77 and after about one quarter mile you will see the parking lot and visitor center on your right.

Broderick Park - Squaw Island

QuikFinder™

Distance	2.5 miles
Direction	NNW
Nearest City/Town	Buffalo
Drivetime	10 minutes

Besides having the distinction of housing a City of Buffalo sewage treatment plant, Squaw Island is home for a little known, but truly loved little park named Broderick Park. It is loved by the fisherman who fish the mighty Niagara River and by those who visit it for its views of the river, Canada and the Peace Bridge.

First Impression

Broderick offers a pleasant respite from city life. A short drive from downtown Buffalo, Broderick is a little oasis bordered by all the classic city trademarks - thruway traffic, a sewage treatment plant and industrial buildings. But look the opposite way and, voila! - the mighty Niagara River, the Peace Bridge and the international views of neighboring Canada are all within sight.

Special Spot

For me, the highlight of Broderick Park is walking the mile and a half long breakwall far out into the river. It is an escape from the city's hassles and personal troubles. And, it is a thrill to walk directly under the Peace Bridge - the international link between the United States and our wonderful neighbor to the north. For something completely different, watch the giant iceflows float by in the spring when the ice boom is removed from the mouth of the Niagara River.

Activities

Walking, picnicking and photography.

Amenities

The park contains a refreshment stand (open during the summer only).

Directions

From downtown Buffalo take Niagara Street north from Niagara Square. Continue on Niagara for about two and one half miles to West Ferry Street. Turn left and drive over the canal across the drawbridge (they really do raise the entire bridge from time to time to let tall ships through the canal - it is quite a sight to see!). Turn left in the park to find the breakwall/walking path.

The remains of a winters worth of ice formed on Lake Erie floats under the Peace Bridge, along the breakwall and past Broderick Park.

Buttermilk Falls of Leroy

One of several waterfalls that plunge over the Onondaga Escarpment. Buttermilk Falls of Leroy (the town name is added to differentiate it from Buttermilk Falls State park) is one of the most spectacular of the Onondaga Escarpment waterfalls. Formed by Oatka Creek on its journey to the Genesee River, these falls are very impressive, rivaling Websters Falls near Hamilton, Ontario (see Spencers Wilderness/Websters Falls later in this book).

QuikFinder™	
Distance	50 miles
Direction	E
Nearest City/Town	Leroy
Drivetime	1 hour

Spray, mist and rainbows delight on a sunny day. As with any waterfall, Buttermilk is most impressive after a heavy rain or during spring melt.

Oatka Creek crashes over Buttermilk Falls on its way to join forces with the Genesee River.

First Impressions

The path to the falls overlook is along an abandoned right of way and is not particularly beautiful. There is an old, crumbling bridge covered with graffiti spanning the creek above the falls and along the path there is a fair amount of trash stuck in the grasses and shrubs. However, the falls more than make up for the neglect of the area. I would love to see this area turned into a park to preserve it for everyone to enjoy and return it to a better state of care.

Special Spot

Climb down one of the trails along the near bank to the creekbed and get as close as you can to the base of the falls (careful, it's very slippery from the mist). You will feel and hear the power of these falls - the wind created by the falling waters drenches you from head to toe with mist and carries with it the awesome roar of great quantities of water slamming into the creekbed below. Also take notice of how some of the water follows invisible channels inside the rock and creates smaller waterfalls to the side that seem to come from nowhere.

Activities

Hiking, nature appreciation, photography.

Amenities

None.

Directions

From downtown Buffalo, access the Niagara Section of the NYS Thruway (Route 190) heading south. After about five miles pick up the mainline NYS Thruway (Route 90) heading east. Stay on Route 90 for approximately 45 miles to exit 47. Exit heading south on Route 19. After about 1.5 miles turn left onto North Street Road. Roughly 100 yards down North Street Road you will see a sharp right turn while straight ahead is a field of gravel and stones. Park here and walk up the gravel road (not far) until you see the abandoned right of way. Turn right and follow the right of way a short distance until you see a path through the woods to the left. Follow the path through the woods and when you emerge from the woods (50 feet or so) you will see a perpendicular path. Follow that path to the right to the overlook of the falls (as you get closer, you will begin to hear the roar of the falls).

Deer Lick Nature Sanctuary

Deer Lick consists of 398 acres of forest, overgrown pasture, and open meadow with 10.5 miles of beautiful hiking trails. In 1967 Deer Lick Nature Sanctuary was designated a Natural Landmark by the U.S. Park Service in recognition of the site as an outstanding example of our Nation's natural heritage. There is something here for all nature lovers - sunny meadows, climax beech, maple and hemlock forest, picture book streams and waterfalls. The Sanctuary area and trails are managed and maintained by The Nature Conservancy.

First Impression

Does not the fact that Deer Lick was designated a Natural Landmark by the U.S. Park Service tell you something about how special it is? There is something almost mystical about the climax forests of Deer Lick... the towering trees, the clear streams and waterfalls, the feeling that nature is in charge here. The first time I entered the forests of Deer Lick, I felt I was entering a special world leaving my troubles behind.

Special Spot

Deer Lick Falls. By following the yellow trail (see trail description below) you will find Deer Lick Creek. At the point where the trail crosses the creek take a short detour downstream along Deer Lick Creek to the overlook of Deer Lick Falls. Accompanied by the sound of the falls and the beauty of the overlook, this is a great meditation spot for those so inclined or just a place to appreciate how special life is.

Activities

Hiking, nature appreciation, photography and cross country skiing and snowshoeing in the winter.

There are five organized trails, each offering something different. At one time the Nature Conservancy kept the register box at the entrance to Deer Lick stocked with trail maps, however, last time I visited there were none. Perhaps they were just temporarily out. Be sure to check. A brief synopsis of the trails follows.

Blue Trail

9/10 of a mile. This trail is hilly and runs through old growth apple trees. Go quietly and keep your eyes open - this is popular deer feeding territory!

Red Trail

1.1 miles. The red trail is an exceptionally pretty trail that encompasses both open meadow and forest along the top of a forested ravine. During the summer into early fall, there is an area along the trail I call the Vine Garden - where the vines have taken over! It's an eerie sight to see - destructive yet beautiful.

Orange Trail

2.1 miles. A predominately hilly, forested trail that runs parallel to Deer Lick Creek.

White Trail

3.2 miles. This trail follows the ridge to Bear Point overlooking the gorge of the south branch of Cattaraugus Creek below (Zoar Valley). The terrain is varied and the trail passes through some impressive sections of climax forest. If you choose to descend

The magic of still half-frozen Deer Lick Falls in early spring.

the trail to the bottom of the gorge, be extremely careful - it is steep and slippery! And be aware that the ascent back up from the gorge is quite strenuous. If you do decide to descend to the canyon floor however, you will be rewarded with the lush and tropical-feeling area simply known as "The Falls" of Zoar Valley (see Zoar Valley - "The Falls" for more information on this area).

Yellow Trail

3.3 miles. This trail descends into a ravine. There is plenty of mature forest to appreciate. You will pass close to Deer Lick Falls as mentioned in the special spot vignette.

Because Deer Lick is adjacent to the Zoar Valley area, you may want to consider visiting one or more of the Zoar Valley sites (see Zoar Valley sites later in this book) while you are in the area.

Numerous activities are prohibited in a nature sanctuary including using motorized vehicles, riding horses, bringing pets, hunting, starting fires, camping, littering or any other activity which would disturb the peace and serenity of the sanctuary. Please observe these prohibitions, they are in the best interests of the sanctuary and of those who visit and respect it.

Amenities

There are two pit toilets at the entrance. There are no other amenities.

Directions

From downtown Buffalo take Route 5 south (The Skyway). Follow Route 5 about 7 miles to Route 75 South. Take Route 75 through Hamburg where it will join with Route 62 (5 miles). Stay on Route 75/62 until Route 62 splits off (about 1.5 miles). Take Route 62 to the Village of Gowanda (about 16 miles). Turn left on S. Water St. (the first street on the extreme left after crossing the bridge) which becomes Commercial St., and then becomes Palmer St. Turn right on Broadway Rd. (less than a mile). Continue on Broadway about one mile then turn left on Point Peter Rd. Make sure you stay on Point Peter Rd. where it bends to the right and Forty Rd. goes straight. Deer Lick is on your left at the crest of a hill about one half mile from the intersection of Forty Rd. and Point Peter Rd.

The Eternal Flame & Falls - Shale Creek Preserve

QuikFinder™

Distance	20 miles
Direction	SE
Nearest City/Town	Orchard Park
Drivetime	25 minutes

CANADA · ONTARIO · ERIE · BUFFALO · PENNSYLVANIA

The Eternal Flame and Falls reside in a gorge in an undeveloped area of Chestnut Ridge Park known as the Shale Creek Preserve. The area is also known as the Seufert Road section or just plain "Seufert" by those who frequent the area. Although the Eternal Flame & Falls gorge area is also accessible from an internal Chestnut Ridge Park road, it is most easily accessed from Seufert Road outside the traditional entrances to the park. This area has been known to birders and nature lovers for years but until now has been a well kept secret from the general public.

The area has mature forest, rolling hills, creeks and steep ravines. There are obvious but unmarked trails. There are remnants of old structures and, near the entrance from Seufert Road, is a piece of an old log that must be five or six feet in diameter! Of course, what really makes this area unique is seeing the "Eternal Flame" burning with water cascading down all around.

The flame itself is caused by natural gas seeping through fissures in the rocks. Despite its name, the flame does occasionally go out during heavy water flow periods and during the winter, but all you need is a lighter or matches to start it again! I have seen the flames vary in size from a few inches to close to a foot high on my visits and a couple of times there were actually two flames burning. The height and number of flames is regulated by the size of the fissures in the rock and the varying pressures of the natural gas storage area below.

The gorge and waterfalls themselves are very picturesque, the flame not withstanding. The water cascades down many layers of shale about 30 feet into the gorge and, as with most waterfalls, is especially impressive after a heavy rain or during the spring snow melt. Keep in mind that during times of heavy water flow it is more than likely that the flame will be extinguished.

Salamanders, or more correctly, red spotted newts can be found under the flat rocks in the gorge. Finding newts is a positive indicator of water and stream health because newts are very sensitive to pollution.

First Impression

Although I had visited Chestnut Ridge many times in the past, I did not discover the Eternal Flame on my own. It can be difficult to find the first time, unless, like I did, you go with a friend who has been there before. Undeveloped and filled with tall trees, graceful streams and cut by deep gorges, Shale Creek is a 'gorge'-ous area that would make quite an impression even if it did not contain the "Eternal Flame".

Special Spot

Paying your respects at the "altar" of the Eternal Flame. There is something almost spiritual about watching the flames dance against the backdrop of the waterfall. It is a unique and special opportunity. The flames provide the best effect in near darkness by bathing the waterfall and gorge in an eerie, flickering glow. However, it can be very difficult and dangerous to try to find your way out of the Preserve in the dark. 'Night vigils' are recommended only if you are going with someone who knows the area well and can easily find the way out with flashlights.

Activities

Hiking, nature appreciation, photography and snowshoeing in the winter.

Amenities

There are no amenities in the Shale Creek Preserve section of the park. Of course, if you visit the developed part of Chestnut Ridge Park, the usual myriad amenities of a county park are available.

Directions

From downtown Buffalo, access the Niagara Section of the NYS Thruway (Route 190) heading south. After about five miles, pick up the mainline NYS Thruway (Route 90) heading west. After a couple more miles pick up Route 219 South. Follow Route 219 for 5 miles and exit at Armor Duells Rd. (Route 240) heading east. Go about 1 mile and turn right on Chestnut Ridge Rd. (Route 277 also known as South Buffalo Rd.). After approximately 3.5 miles, turn right on Seufert Rd. Several hundred feet from the corner you will see a heavy metal gate on the right hand side. Park along the road and hike in. Follow the most obvious trail always bearing left. You will descend in and out of several small ravines before reaching a point high above the main gorge where you can hear the water splashing down the shale cascade below. The path will then descend sharply until you reach the creek. Turn left in the creekbed and follow the creek to the falls. The flame may not be lit if there has been heavy water flow or it is wintertime. You can usually re-start the flame with matches or a cigarette lighter. Be careful around the falls, the rocks are slippery!

Heavy water flow had extinguished the "Eternal Flame" on this late winter day.

Evangola State Park

An expansive, natural beach along the shores of Lake Erie. The beach is long - great for strolling along the shoreline. The sunsets can be spectacular, especially on clear, humid summer nights or when broken clouds are gathered on the horizon. The remainder of the park is extensive and has plenty of open space for just about any type of recreational activity imaginable.

QuikFinder™

Distance	25 miles
Direction	SW
Nearest City/Town	Angola
Drivetime	40 minutes

CANADA

ONTARIO

ERIE

BUFFALO

PENNSYLVANIA

The sunset paints the waters of Lake Erie with brilliant color.

33

First Impression

I could not imagine why there were not more people in the park. Evangola has everything - an expansive, natural beach (a little rocky, but hey, it's natural), plenty of picnic and recreation area, killer sunsets, camping, a bathhouse, a snack bar - what more could you ask for? Maybe the reason I thought there were so few people in the park is because Evangola is so large that it can accommodate many people without feeling overcrowded.

Special Spot

The beach. The beach is long - I would guess nearly a mile long. There are plenty of things to see - unusually shaped driftwood, carved out bluffs, beach flora and plenty of interesting rocks for the beachcomber. And good for people watching - if that's what 'floats your boat'. The beach is long and wide enough so that it never feels crowded even on a hot summer weekend day.

Stay until the end of the day for a renowned Lake Erie sunset. The sky over the lake is interesting in all types of weather, often changing quickly. And because the sun sets over the lake, there are no obstacles to obstruct the view.

Activities

Many types of recreational activities are possible here - swimming, rollerblading, baseball, soccer, picnicking, beach walking, nature appreciation, photography, sunbathing, bicycling, jogging and cross-country skiing and snowshoeing in the winter Evangola is so expansive it accommodates almost any type of activity imaginable.

Amenities

The bathhouse is much more than a bathhouse. It contains a snack bar, changing rooms and public restrooms. Public restroom buildings are also scattered about the park. There are more than enough picnic tables and grills for picnicking on even the most crowded days. Also on the grounds are baseball diamonds and a soccer field.

The campgrounds are accessed by a separate entrance.   The campgrounds share the beach and facilities. Call Evangola State Park at 549-1760 for more information on camping.

Directions

From downtown Buffalo, take Route 5 south for about 24 miles. You will see the signs directing you into the park. There is an entrance fee charged during the summer season until 4 PM each day.

Forest Lawn Cemetery

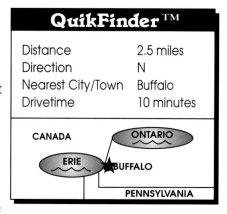

A grand old cemetery located in the heart of the City of Buffalo. Lush, rolling, quiet - a true respite from city life. Yes, it is a cemetery but also a whole lot more. Huge old oak, maple and beech trees form a leafy canopy over some of Western New York's most famous historical dignitaries buried at their feet. Ponds, stone bridges and walls and a creek with a small set of waterfalls flowing through the middle of the cemetery help further the feeling of country in the city. Great horned owls live here along with ducks, geese, songbirds and plenty of squirrels and chipmunks.

Forest Lawn is a Buffalo historic landmark. Many of the "movers and shakers" of Buffalo history are buried here. My purpose here is to introduce you to Forest Lawn and the pleasures of a visit. By doing only that, I am merely scratching the surface of what Forest Lawn means to Buffalo. For more in-depth information about Forest Lawn and its history, I recommend going to your local bookstore and picking up a copy of **Forest Lawn Cemetery: Buffalo History Preserved** - published by the Forest Lawn Heritage Foundation.

First Impression

I felt like I had driven through a secret gate taking me into a hidden oasis. Forest Lawn is meticulously maintained with dozens of varieties of trees, shrubs and flowers. It almost has the feel of an old southern plantation with its stately majestic trees and well groomed, lush appearance. The first time I drove in I knew I had found a lunchtime escape from the corporate world.

Special Spot

I feel I must mention two Special Spots here. The first and obvious choice is Mirror Pond. Mirror Pond is a peaceful, stone-lined pond surrounded by fruit and ornamental trees and populated by ducks and geese. Mirrored in the center is a beautiful sculpture and fountain entitled 'The Three Graces'. Visit Mirror Pond in the spring when all the trees are in bloom or fall when the leaves have turned color for a special treat.

The second is Serenity Falls. While diminutive relative to other waterfalls mentioned in this book, they are grand for the escape they represent from the city life just outside the cemetery gates. When you are next to the falls, all traces of the city are gone - all you can see is the falls and all you can hear is the water. During the summer an unidentified plant gives the whole falls area a delicious aroma completing the country-in-the-city feel.

A Special Spot honorable mention must go to the stone with one of my favorite poems carved into it:

Sanctum

I built a tiny garden
In a corner of my heart
I kept it just for lovely things
And bade all else depart
And ever there was music
And flowers blossomed fair
Yet never was it perfect
Until you entered there
- *By Beulah B. Malkin*

Mirror Pond lives up to its name.

Activities

Walking, jogging, biking, roller blading, carry-in picnicking (no fires or cooking), reading, meditating - anything peaceful, quiet and non-offensive. This is a wonderful setting for creativity - I have seen artists painting and sketching, writers creating new worlds with their words, photographers capturing the spirit of the place on film, and even actors practicing their lines!

Which way is up? The tranquil water reflects two prime features of Forest Lawn.

In addition to the above, there are self guided tours, organized tours and trolley rides available at certain times of the year. For more information on tours, call Forest Lawn at 885-1600 or stop at the Information Center just inside the Delaware Avenue gates.

Amenities

There are public restrooms near the Delaware Avenue entrance. Benches can be found around Mirror Pond and strategically placed in other scenic spots around Forest Lawn.

Directions

From downtown Buffalo, head north on Delaware Avenue for approximately two miles to the intersection with Delevan Avenue. Just past Delevan Avenue on your right you will see massive, wrought iron entrance gates.

There is also an entrance off Main Street. Just past the intersection with Delevan Avenue (heading north from downtown) turn left and enter through the wrought iron gates.

Mirror Pond can be found easily by entering from Delaware Avenue and following the main road (the road with the painted lines on it) to just before it crosses a stone bridge. Turn right here. You should be paralleling Scajaquada Creek with the creek on your left. After making the turn, you will see Mirror Pond almost immediately.

Serenity Falls is most easily found from the Main Street entrance. Upon entering through the gates, turn left. At the first fork, turn right. Not far from the turn, you will see a small parking area just before the bridge over Scajaquada Creek. You will see a small sign that says "Serenity Falls". You can view the falls from the side of the bridge. To get up close and personal to the falls, park your car and walk across the bridge. Once across the bridge, turn right and walk along the bank until you see the paths down to the creek.

To find the stone with the poem "Sanctum" carved into it, enter from the Main Street entrance. Turn left and stay left at the first fork, following the road that parallels Delevan Avenue. Several hundred feet from the first fork is another road to the right. The stone sits off the right hand side of the road immediately after that intersection.

For other information or directions, stop at the Visitors Center located just inside the Delaware Avenue gates. There is also a large map of the grounds near the Delaware Avenue entrance.

Genesee Road County Forest

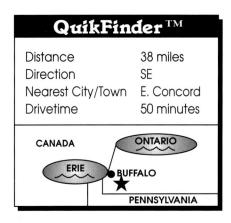

QuikFinder™

Distance	38 miles
Direction	SE
Nearest City/Town	E. Concord
Drivetime	50 minutes

CANADA
ONTARIO
ERIE
BUFFALO
PENNSYLVANIA

During the great depression, farmers were forced to abandon or sell their land to the county. This was because of economic factors and the difficulty of producing an acceptable yield using the farming methods of the day combined with a relatively short growing season. To provide jobs, the government then hired the unemployed to replant the land with trees. This is how the Genesee Road County Forest came to be.

First Impressions

I was surprised and delighted by the amount of maintained trails throughout the forest. The trails feature quaint, wooden walk bridges made on premises with wood from the Forest. Picnic tables and benches likewise constructed are scattered throughout. Parts of the forest where replanted with pines struck me as almost eerie; the combined effect of the quiet underfoot from the thick bed of needles and the almost complete blockage of sunlight from the tightness of the canopy above makes for a surreal feel.

Special Spot

The wooden bridges over the streams are storybook. Near one of the bridges there is a small meadow with a picnic table - this is a particularly nice spot for a romantic lunch.

Activities

Hiking, picnicking, nature appreciation, photography and cross-country skiing and snowshoeing in the winter.

Every time, while visiting during the winter to cross-country ski or snowshoe, I have been delighted by a toasty warm fire in the woodstove of the warm-up building maintained by Forestry Bureau employees.

At certain times of the year there are sawmill and maple production demonstrations on the premises. Call the Erie County Forestry Bureau at 496-7410 for more information.

Amenities

Public restrooms, a warm-up building with a wood stove, and a picnic shelter. Picnic tables and benches are scattered throughout.

Directions

From downtown Buffalo, access the Niagara Section of the NYS Thruway (Route 190) heading south. After about five miles, pick up the mainline NYS Thruway (Route 90) heading west. After a couple of miles, pick up Route 219 South. Follow Route 219 for about 20 miles and exit at Genesee Road. Follow Genesee Road east (turn left) for about 7 miles and look for the County Forest buildings on your left. The forest is on both sides of the road.

One of the charming rustic footbridges crossing a tributary of Cazenovia Creek.

Glen Falls Park

Glen Falls Park is a small and relatively unknown park nestled into the hustle and bustle that is Williamsville. Small in size, it is big on beauty. The highlight of the park is Glen Falls, where Ellicott Creek plunges over the Onondaga Escarpment. The park also features ponds, ducks, footpaths and is overlooked by a landmark, the historic Williamsville Water Mill.

QuikFinder™

Distance	10 miles
Direction	NE
Nearest City/Town	Williamsville
Drivetime	20 minutes

CANADA   ONTARIO   ERIE   ★ BUFFALO   PENNSYLVANIA

The Historic Williamsville Water Mill

41

First Impressions

When I was a boy, I visited the site often when it was the Glen Park amusement park. I would bicycle to the park and spend hours exploring the creek and surrounding areas. The park still delights me. The design makes it feel larger than it really is and it provides an effective escape from busy Main Street just a few hundred yards away. Whenever I am in the area I visit the park for a "soul-refresher".

Special Spot

Sitting on the bench next to the waterfalls. The falls are impressive even during the summer due to the good year-round water volume of Ellicott Creek. The roar of the water as it tumbles down the escarpment effectively shuts out the sounds of civilization and provides an escape from the commotion of everyday life.

Activities

Walking, nature appreciation, photography. Historic old Williamsville borders the south side of the park and features several original buildings including the red Water Mill. Old Williamsville is fun to wander around while trying to imagine what it must have been like when the William's Mill was first built in 1811.

Amenities

Public restrooms in the east parking lot.

Directions

From downtown Buffalo, take Main Street (Route 5) east about 10 miles into the village of Williamsville. Turn left on North Cayuga Road, then take the second right onto Glen Avenue. There are two parking lots on the left, one before and one after the bridge over Ellicott Creek. The falls are across the street from the parking areas.

Alternatively, from downtown Buffalo, access the Niagara Section of the NYS Thruway (Route 190) heading south. About five miles, pick up the mainline NYS Thruway (Route 90) heading east. After about five miles, exit onto Route 290 (Youngmann Expressway) heading west. Exit almost immediately onto Route 5 - Main St. heading east. After a little over a mile turn left onto North Cayuga Rd. then take the second right onto Glen Avenue. There are two parking lots on the left, one before and one after the bridge over Ellicott Creek. The falls are across the street from the parking areas.

Griffis Sculpture Park

A 400-acre park opened by Larry Griffis in the late 60's to display his awesome metal works of art. The soul of the surrounding forest adds tremendously to the spirit of his works. The forest also effectively separates the sculptures from one another, allowing each one to be appreciated individually.

The park primarily features Larry Griffis' sculptures and creations (although other artists do have a presence). Most of the works are constructed of metal and are larger than life. They are displayed on hillsides, in open meadows and in the forest. These sculptures are incredible works of art the likes of which you may have never seen if you have not been fortunate enough to visit Griffis Sculpture Park! You will see giant insects, huge 'Amazon' women, miniature castles and truly abstract objects. Children love Griffis Park because they can climb on, in and around the sculptures without parents worrying that they may be damaging them. The park is in three sections all with hiking trails. There are separate road accesses and parking areas for each section.

The park also features two ponds adorned by sculptures, one of which has a contingent of geese and swans who take up residence from spring to fall. In the largest section of the park there is a performance stage where occasional music concerts and performances are held. What a great setting for a show!

First Impression

The very first time I drove through the Rohr Hill section of the park I did not know what to expect. I could not quite visualize the giant metal 'Amazon' women, larger-than-life animals and huge insects that I was told I would see. It was almost dark as I entered and I could not believe what my eyes were seeing in the fading light. Two huge surreal women with dangling earrings and possibly African headdresses were silhouetted against the night sky, one on each side of the road. It seemed they were guarding the Park. Next I spotted what appeared to be the royalty of the Park - a King, Queen and Bishop. On the opposite side are several 'Amazon' women who must be at least 20 feet tall. My first experience in Griffis Park was both magical and mystical and these attributes have lured me back time and time again.

An 'Amazon' woman thunders through the dawn woods of Griffis Sculpture Park

Special Spot

There are so many... forced to choose I would be roaming the woods to the rear of the Rohr Rd. (as opposed to the Rohr Hill Rd.) section. There are sculptures lurking throughout and the forest seems to come alive with their presence. There are meditation circles, busts of what appears to be multicultural

Above - Young and old delight in climbing around in the Griffis castle

imaginary famous people and all kinds of other unusual and haunting sculptures nestled into this fanciful forest. There are also plenty of good hiking trails that go deep into the woods.

One of the 'guards' of the Rohr Hill Rd. section of the park

Activities

Hiking, art and nature appreciation, photography, carry-in, carry-out picnicking (no fires) and in the winter, cross-country skiing and snowshoeing. The park is free but please donate something to help support the Ashford Hollow Foundation that maintains the park and supports other creative endeavors.

For more information about Griffis Park, contact the Ashford Hollow Foundation office at 886-3616.

Amenities

Pit toilets.

Directions

From downtown Buffalo, access the Niagara section of the NYS Thruway (Route 190) heading south. After about five miles, pick up the mainline NYS Thruway (Route 90) heading west. After another couple of miles pick up Route 219 South. Follow Route 219 until the expressway section of it ends at Springville. Turn left, then right and continue on the surface section of Route 219 for about seven miles to Ahrens Road on your right (there is a small sign). Drive up the hill and turn left at Rohr Hill Rd. Now keep your eyes open, soon the fantastical materializations of Larry Griffis' visions will come into view! To get to the other main section of the park, continue on Rohr Hill Rd. until you reach Rohr Rd. (first right - there is a sign). About one mile from the turn on your right you will see the signs for the Sculpture Park. Drive in, park, enjoy and don't forget to donate something! To access the other, less developed section of the park - from Route 219 - turn right on Ahrens Rd. but instead of turning left at Rohr Hill Rd. continue straight on Prill Rd. Shortly thereafter on your left you will see a clearing with some trails. Park here and hike in. To return to Route 219, just turn around and head straight down the hill (Prill Rd. to Ahrens Rd. to Route 219).

Note - Rohr Hill Road is a seasonal use only road (not plowed during the winter). Rohr Rd. can also be accessed from Prill Rd., about two miles from the intersection with Ahrens Rd.

Letchworth - in Winter!

A winter wonderland! The gorge is cloaked in snow. Waterfalls are frozen into ice art. There are quiet and peaceful trails for cross-country skiing or snowshoeing. This is the Letchworth you already know in a whole new set of gorgeous snow-white clothes without the crowds.

QuikFinder™	
Distance	55 miles
Direction	ESE
Nearest City/Town	Castile
Drivetime	1-1/2 hours

CANADA · ONTARIO · ERIE · BUFFALO · PENNSYLVANIA

First Impression

Mother Nature, the artist at her best. Beautiful snow covered scenery. Very few people. Wildlife and nature back in charge. Spectacular Letchworth with a kind of a hush over it looking very different than in the other three seasons.

Special Spot

Treasuring the view of the frozen falls. The incredible ice shapes and forms sculpted by the spray and falling water and the plumes of frigid water bursting through the ice are truly sublime sights.

Activities

Cross country skiing, snowshoeing, nature appreciation, photography. Avoid the portion of the park open to snowmobiles if you relish peace and quiet.

Amenities

Winterized cabins are available for rent in the park.

Directions

From downtown Buffalo, access the Niagara Section of the NYS Thruway (Route 190) heading south. After about five miles pick up the mainline NYS Thruway (Route 90) heading west. Stay to your right and pick up Route 400 South. After about eleven miles, exit at Route 20A headed east (away from the village of East Aurora). After approximately 23 miles, turn right on Route 19. Follow Route 19 about 5 miles to where 19 and 19A split. Take 19A for about 6 miles and turn left on Route 39. Look for and follow the signs into the park.

Right - Frigid water manages to burst through the ice-encrusted falls at the height of winter in Letchworth State Park.

Letchworth Winter Wonderland

Little Rock City

Little Rock City (LRC) is an amazing example of the dozens of 'rock cities' scattered about the hills of the southern tier of Western New York and Northwestern Pennsylvania. With some boulders larger than houses and a system of eerily straight streets and alleyways, LRC does feel like a prehistoric city of stone. You almost expect Fred and Barney to come strolling around the next corner!

QuikFinder™

Distance	60 miles
Direction	S
Nearest City/Town	Ellicottville
Drivetime	1-1/2 hours

CANADA · ONTARIO · ERIE · BUFFALO · PENNSYLVANIA

The 'City' is rich in ferns, lichens and mosses. Some beds of moss are so soft and thick that you might be tempted to take a little nap on one after some serious hiking. Another vegetative highlight is the multitude of massive root systems clinging to the sides

A street between buildings in Little Rock City.

of the boulders looking like plant octopi. These root systems are sent down by trees above sometimes up to thirty feet in search of water and nutrients in the soil below.

LRC (and all the other 'rock cities') are actually a layer of erosion resistant rock which, over time, split apart and now appear to be completely separate huge boulders. Without knowledge of how they were formed, one can only imagine the legends prehistoric man must have passed down for generations about these areas.

First Impression

When I tried to find LRC for the first time some twenty years ago, I couldn't. What I did not know at the time was that the City is situated on a hillside lower than the road and therefore is not visible from the road! Armed with a better understanding of what to look for, I had better luck finding it the next time and have enjoyed introducing many others to the wonders of LRC ever since.

When I finally did find LRC, my first impression was one of childlike wonderment and curiosity (one heck-of-a-place to play hide and go seek!) Not knowing my way around, I was a little uncomfortable about being able to find my way back. But, being an explorer by nature, I plunged into the LRC maze and easily found my way back out.

Special Spot

Because all of Little Rock City is unique and special, I decided rather than select a spot, I would choose a season as special. I have chosen winter. However, before I launch into my description of winter in LRC, I must impress on you that I do not recommend anyone exploring during the winter unless you are experienced with long distance cross country skiing or showshoeing. The access to LRC is by seasonal use only roads (not plowed) and the snow is generally too deep for even four wheel drive vehicles. Visit spring through fall, it's plenty delightful then!

Like Letchworth, in the winter LRC takes on a whole new personality. Rock overhangs become ice caves complete with freestanding 'ice walls'. Rock faces are covered with sculptured ice sometimes two or three feet thick. Icicles and ice pillars abound - small, medium and even large columns sometimes twenty feet tall or more! It is fascinating to see LRC in the winter, especially after visits during the other three seasons.

Activities

Hiking, picnicking, nature appreciation, photography and cross-country skiing and snowshoeing in the winter.

There are two trails in LRC:

The *Nature Trail* is a short trail entirely within LRC. It is marked with pink blazes.

The *Conservation Trail* traverses LRC and continues both north and south. The Conservation Trail is marked with white and orange blazes.

Amenities

The Department of Environmental Conservation has installed several picnic shelters complete with tables.

Directions

From downtown Buffalo, access the Niagara Section of the NYS Thruway (Route 190) heading south. After about five miles pick up the mainline NYS Thruway (Route 90) heading west. After another couple of miles pick up Route 219 south. Follow Route 219 to Springville until the expressway section ends. Turn left, then right and continue on the surface section of Route 219 for about 17 miles through the Village of Ellicottville. At the traffic light at the end of the village, go straight on Route 242. Do not turn left on Route 219. Follow Route 242 for about 3 miles to Whig Street and turn left. The first mile and a half of Whig Street is a forest road and is not maintained (plowed) during the winter. Continue on Whig Street (becomes paved) past Mutton Hollow. Less than a mile past Mutton Hollow on the left is Hungry Hollow. After several hundred yards, Hungry Hollow becomes a seasonal use road and is also not maintained during the winter. Do not attempt to drive this road with a low clearance vehicle, this road can be full of ruts and washouts. Follow Hungry Hollow about one mile to Rock City Rd. (the first right). Drive Rock City Rd. to the end circle. Park well off the side of the circle. The 'City' is on your left as you enter the circle. The 'City' is not immediately obvious because the road is at the same level or higher than the rocks. You will be descending down into the city. Look around until you discover the path down into LRC. Once there, you can explore on your own or follow one of the trails. I recommend exploring for a while then finding a trail when you are ready to return. Do not worry, heading uphill will always get you back to the road (just remember that the road is higher than the 'city').

Ice Caves await the intrepid winter visitor to Little Rock City.

Spencers Wilderness Gorge: Websters Falls & Tews Falls

QuikFinder™

Distance	75 miles
Direction	NW
Nearest City/Town	Hamilton
Drivetime	1-1/2 hours

Just outside of the cities of Hamilton and Dundas, Ontario, lies a relatively unknown gorge containing two spectacular waterfalls. The falls are formed by Spencer Creek and a tributary spilling over the Niagara Escarpment.

Tews Falls disappearing into the ice mountain below.

The two creeks join further downstream and flow through the beautiful Spencers Wilderness Gorge on the way to their final discharge into Lake Ontario.

Websters Falls and Tews Falls are two more in the series of spectacular waterfalls in the Niagara Region. Tews Falls is the third highest unimpeded straight drop falls in the area after Taughannock and Niagara respectively. Websters Falls has a great deal of volume and its power is quite impressive during periods of heavy water flow. To have these two incredible waterfalls so close that you can easily walk from one to the other is our good fortune!

First Impression

As mentioned above, Websters Falls has the higher volume of the two falls - very impressive indeed. My first visit was in early April during the spring snow melt. The thundering crash of the falls was sending up huge billows of mist which, over the winter, had frozen into fascinating ice sculptures.

What Tews Falls lacks in volume it makes up for in height - an over 130 foot straight drop. As with Websters Falls, my first visit was in early April and there was still a substantial ice mountain at the base of the falls. In fact, the ice had built up so high that the bottom 30 feet or so of the waterfalls disappeared into a large hole in the ice mountain!

The gorge itself is surprisingly pristine, wild and scenic - especially considering its proximity to one of Ontario's larger, more industrial cities. Filled with huge boulders and maintained in a natural state, I felt like I was hiking along a stream in the Adirondacks, not just outside of Hamilton, Ontario.

Special Spot

Approaching either set of falls from inside the gorge. Hiking to them through the gorge allows you to appreciate the considerable natural beauty of the whole area. Also, the falls are much more impressive when viewed (and heard and felt) at the base.

Activities

Hiking, picnicking, photography, nature appreciation.

There is a connecting trail between the Websters Falls and Tews Falls areas. This trail is part of the **Bruce Trail**. The Bruce Trail runs from Queenston (Niagara Region) to the end of the Bruce Peninsula (which forms part of the western boundary of the Georgian Bay). The Bruce Trail is marked with white blazes (there are unmarked local trails also).

Amenities

Picnic tables, restrooms.

Directions

From downtown Buffalo, access the Niagara Section of the NYS Thruway (Route 190) heading north. Follow the signs to the Peace Bridge and enter Canada. As you proceed from the customs area take the Queen Elizabeth Way (QEW) north. Drive about 63 miles on the QEW and exit onto Route 403 West (past Hamilton and just after the Burlington Bay Skyway Bridge). Take Route 403 approximately 6 miles and exit onto Route 8 heading west. Then you have two options - hike to the falls through the gorge or drive to the falls. The directions continue below for either option.

(1) *Hike through Spencers Gorge to the base of either falls* - follow Route 8 out of Dundas up a steep grade. Turn right about halfway up the grade immediately after passing under a railroad bridge. There is a gated entrance to the parking area. If closed, pull off to the side, park and walk in. Otherwise, pull in to the parking area and park your car. Look for the white blazes of the Bruce Trail. Follow the trail into the gorge. At the bottom of the gorge, turn left and follow the trail to Websters Falls. On your way, you will see a side canyon on the opposite side of the gorge. That canyon leads to the base of Tews Falls. Depending on the time of year and the amount of water flow, you may or may not be able to cross the creek to get to the side canyon.

(2) *Drive to the falls* - follow Route 8 out of the City of Dundas, up a steep hill. At the top of the hill, look for Webster Lane on your right. Park and walk in. If no parking is available, continue straight (do not turn left when Route 8 does, but rather continue straight on Brock Rd.). Turn right at the next intersection on Harvest Rd. Follow Harvest Rd. to the parking area for Tews Falls on your right. A connecting trail links both the Websters Falls and Tews Falls observation areas.

The 'Ice-Gods' of Webster Falls.

Zoar Valley - Overview

Zoar Valley is an awesome canyon carved out by the waters of Cattaraugus Creek as it snakes through the hills of southern Erie and northern Cattaraugus counties. All told, there is about 7 miles of gorge contained within the designated State Forest area. Zoar Valley remains widely unknown despite its rugged and untamed beauty. A description of a few of the main features that help make Zoar Valley such an extraordinary place follows.

QuikFinder™

Distance	35 miles
Direction	S
Nearest City/Town	Gowanda
Drivetime	1 hour

CANADA ONTARIO ERIE BUFFALO PENNSYLVANIA

Mist cloaks Cattaraugus Creek on a cool morning in Zoar Valley.

Second deepest gorge

The second deepest gorge in Western New York - over 400 feet deep in sections. Only Letchworth is deeper.

Spectacular scenery

Towering cliffs, knife-edge ridges, waterfalls, exposed rock strata, swimming holes, abundant and lush flora and fauna make Zoar Valley a nature lover's delight.

Waterfalls galore

As creeks and streams feed the gorge they plunge down the vertical rock walls creating dozens of variously sized and shaped waterfalls. An early spring raft trip through the canyon is the best way to see the spectacular array of waterfalls in full flow.

Nudist beach

One of only a handful of places where you can shed all of your clothes and not worry about being arrested. Entire families in the buff hold hands and stroll through the canyon. Talk about growing up au naturel!

Raw wilderness

Due to its remoteness, very few people visit the area. If there were more than a couple hundred people in the entire gorge area on the hottest of summer weekend days, it would be surprising. Away from the creekbed nearest the parking areas, the trails, and the most scenic spots, I would wager that Zoar Valley has some of the least oft visited areas (by humans anyway) in Western New York - great places to 'get away from it all'!

Wildlife galore

On a recent hiking trip down the canyon, my companion and I encountered the following wildlife:

- Hawks
- Turkey Vultures
- an American Woodcock (one strange looking bird)
- dozens of Red Spotted Newts
- A Bullfrog

- a Canada Goose couple with chicks bobbing downstream

- two Great Blue Herons

- an assortment of songbirds

- a Fawn, no more than two weeks old, stranded on a rock ledge

The fawn was surrounded by rushing water with nowhere to go. Apparently, it had been caught in the high waters resulting from the torrential rainfall the previous night and had struggled to make its way through the rushing waters to the ledge. With its youthful ungainly gait, it had not been able to follow its mother. It was exhausted and hungry.

We could find no footprints in the sand that would indicate that the mother was to be found. This area was completely isolated by high water and we were afraid the fawn would not survive. My companion is training to be a wildlife rehabilitator, so we decided to rescue the fawn. We brought it out of the canyon and to a qualified deer rehabilitation specialist. Yes, the fawn has completely recovered and is back leaping through forest and field!

First Impression

See the 'First Impression', 'Special Spot', and 'Activities' sections for each individual area following.

Amenities

None

Directions (All Areas)

From downtown Buffalo take Route 5 south (The Skyway). Follow Route 5 about 7 miles to Route 75 South. Take Route 75 through Hamburg where it joins with Route 62 (5 miles). Stay on Route 75/62 until Route 62 splits off (about 1.5 miles). Take Route 62 south. Follow directions below for each individual area.

To The Falls

Take Route 62 into the village of Gowanda (about 16 miles). Turn left on S. Water St. (the first street on the extreme left after crossing the bridge) which becomes Commercial St., and then Palmer St. Turn right on Broadway Rd. (less than a mile). Continue on Broadway about one mile, then turn left on Point Peter Rd. Follow Point Peter to Forty Rd. (stay left - Point Peter veers right) and follow the steep hill down to the parking lot at the bottom. Park, climb into the valley. Hike to your right (south) following the creek for 30 to 60 minutes (depending on your hiking speed) and it will be obvious

The exhausted fawn had all but given up.

Other wildlife 'hanging around' Zoar Valley.

when you reach the falls. Do not be fooled by the smallish waterfalls streaming down the sides of the canyon - 'The Falls' is part of the creek itself. Alternatively, you can reach the falls area through the Deer Lick Nature Preserve (see the "White Trail" description in the separate section on Deer Lick).

To the Knife Edge Ridge

Take Route 62 into the village of Gowanda (about 16 miles). In Gowanda, turn left on Gowanda-Zoar Rd. just before the bridge over Cattaraugus Creek. Follow Gowanda-Zoar Rd. about three miles and turn right on Unger. Follow Unger until it ends. Turn left (Vail Rd.). Immediately on your right you will see the "State Forest" sign and entrance road. Pull in and park. Hike the access road to the edge of the canyon (look for the powerlines crossing the canyon in front of you). Turn right and follow the path into the woods along the canyon's edge. After a few minutes you will see a large boulder in the path. Look to your left. This is Knife Edge Ridge.

To Valentine Flats and 'The Point'

Take Route 62 into the village of Gowanda (about 16 miles). Turn left on S. Water St. (the first street on the extreme left after crossing the bridge) which becomes Commercial St., and then Palmer St. Turn right on Broadway Rd. (less than a mile). Continue on Broadway about one mile, then turn left on Point Peter Rd. Proceed about one-half mile and turn left on Valentine Flats Rd. Follow the road to the dead end and park in the parking area. Hike in straight on the old road and then hang left at the edge of the gorge. Follow the obvious path out to 'The Point'. You will know when you've reached it.....

To get to the 'flats' turn right at the edge of the gorge. Again, the path is well worn and obvious, but be careful, it can be slippery and wet, even in the summer. Follow the path down into the valley and across the 'Flats' to the creek.

Zoar Valley - 'The Falls'

QuikFinder ™

Distance	35 miles
Direction	S
Nearest City/Town	Gowanda
Drivetime	1 hour

Known simply as 'The Falls' because they are the only significant falls in Zoar Valley actually on either branch of Cattaraugus Creek. All the other falls in Zoar Valley are formed by tributaries descending the steep walls of the gorge. 'The Falls' crash into a sizeable swimming hole into which the daring dive or jump from above. Just downstream, there is another swimming hole with a 'Tarzan' rope attached to a tree overhanging the water. The feeling of the entire falls area is one of a southwest canyon with its steep rock walls and water chiseled channels through the bedrock. The only thing missing is the red color in the rock.

First Impression

Rugged. Lush. Almost tropical. I had hiked in the Zoar Valley area several times before I encountered the falls, so I was familiar with the rugged beauty of the area. Finding the falls was the icing on the cake. When I saw the falls area for the first time, I was amazed - here was a remote, virtually unknown, wild and natural canyon right here in Western New York just an hour south of Buffalo. This certainly wasn't the Western New York that most people know!

Special Spot

The Falls. In the summer, young daredevils dive or jump from the top of the falls into the swimming hole below. Another challenge, for those who don't mind subjecting themselves to the pounding of the water from above, is to slip behind the falls into the small cave. The area above the falls has a large, flat, natural rock beach area on which to lay down a towel and catch some rays. On a hot summer day there can be a no more glorious place to be!

Activities

Hiking, swimming, tubing, rafting, canoeing, nature appreciation, photography.

Amenities, Directions

See the Zoar Valley - Overview section.

Special Note

Please pack out what you pack in. Nothing ruins beautiful scenery like trash.

Beyond Buffalo!

Right - Do you dare descend the Knife Edge Ridge?

'The Falls' of Zoar Valley.

Zoar Valley - The Knife Edge

The 'Knife Edge' is a ridge that extends from the north rim of Zoar Valley into the canyon descending nearly 400 feet. From the top of the 'Knife Edge' the views are spectacular - you can see far upstream and down and admire the awesome etched cliff faces of the south wall at the same time.

QuikFinder ™

Distance	35 miles
Direction	S
Nearest City/Town	Gowanda
Drivetime	1 hour

CANADA   ONTARIO

ERIE   BUFFALO

PENNSYLVANIA

First Impression

At the top of the 'Knife Edge', plant life struggles to survive. The result is stunted growth and sparse vegetation creating an otherworldly feel. The views are simply astounding. The first time I saw it, I was transported somewhere else in the world or maybe even to some distant planet where life also exists. My first impression was that this place was so enchanting that I would need to come back again for a second impression and again for a third and again...

Special Spot

Standing at the top of the 'Knife Edge' enjoying the 180 degree views of the canyon stretching far into the distance. For a special treat, visit in early summer just after dawn when the trees, shrubs and grasses are still bathed in dew. You will delight in some of the most delicious natural perfumes Mother Nature has to offer.

Activities

Hiking, nature appreciation, photography and, in the winter, snowshoeing .

Hike past the 'Knife Edge' on the rim trail and you will be rewarded with more valley panoramas, a waterfall overlook and the privilege of wandering among rare old growth trees.

Morning calm along the 'Flats'.

Amenities, Directions

See the Zoar Valley - Overview section.

65

Zoar Valley - Valentine Flats

QuikFinder™

Distance	35 miles
Direction	S
Nearest City/Town	Gowanda
Drivetime	1 hour

CANADA
ONTARIO
ERIE
BUFFALO
PENNSYLVANIA

The 'Flats' area is famous for being an all summer season long 'Hippie' settlement each year back in the sixties. At that time, the road extended right down into the canyon and the Hippies would drive down in and camp for the entire summer. Who could blame them? Gorgeous canyon scenery, great swimming, a lush meadow to settle into and a complete escape from civilization!

As a result of the abuse the area took from garbage and human waste, overnight camping has since been prohibited in the canyon area. The original road is washed out and the only way into the 'Flats' is to hike in. If you explore the base of the ridge along which the trail descends into the valley, you can find an upside-down car that didn't quite make it!

First Impression

Paradise! Almost everything you could possibly want on a hot summer day is here - swimming, lush canyon scenery and a nudist beach to top it off! Yes, my first impression was surprise at seeing the nudists - men, women, even whole families!

Special Spot

Where the south and the main branch of Cattaraugus Creek meet. There are several natural beaches here and a great tubing run. This is one of the most popular summer 'hangout' spots in Zoar Valley. It is so beautiful here - just bring your food and beverages and you will never want to leave!

Activities

Hiking, swimming, tubing, canoeing, nature appreciation, photography.

Amenities, Directions

See the Zoar Valley - Overview section.

Daytrippers

Allegany State Park

Allegany State Park is a rugged and scenic piece of the Appalachian Mountains in southern Cattaraugus County. At 67,000 acres, it is the largest state park (the Adirondacks and Catskills are Forest Preserves) in New York. It contains a treasure trove of mountain foothills, lakes, streams, wildlife, forests (including the largest tract of old growth forest known in Western New York) and plenty of undisturbed nature.

QuikFinder™

Distance	75 miles
Direction	S
Nearest City/Town	Salamanca
Drivetime	2 hours

While many people are aware of Allegany, I decided to include it because it is the crown jewel of the New York State Parks system and it is so diverse - there is something here for every type of outdoor enthusiast. Also, it is the single largest tract of relatively undisturbed wilderness in New York west of the Adirondack and Catskill Forest Preserves.

The Administration building nestled into the vast forests of Allegany.

Red House Lake at dawn.

Beyond Buffalo!

First Impression

As a child, my parents introduced me to nature and wilderness through annual week-long family camp outings in the western Adirondacks (the Stillwater/Beaver River area - see *Weekenders*). Until I discovered Allegany, I believed that I had to travel to the Adirondacks for that type of experience!

The first time I drove into Allegany State Park I knew I had found paradise in Western New York. No matter where you enter the park, it immediately feels intensely different from the surrounding area. Allegany is roughly 100 square miles of rugged forested hillsides, undisturbed creeks and streams, huge, old growth trees and is populated by bears, deer, beaver, turkey, porcupines and myriad small creatures. All this is complemented by tastefully constructed cabins and facilities, most located near the two beautiful lakes.

Special Spot

Allegany is far too large and diverse to cover all of its special spots, so I am covering a few I find *especially* compelling.

The Hiking Trails

Not including old logging roads and dirt roads, there are over 70 miles of marked hiking trails and *every* one is delightful. Some feature ascents to spectacular vistas, others skirt rock formations such as the 'bear caves', some are perfect for cross country skiing and *every* one features beautiful forest scenery.

Thunder Rocks

One of the many 'rock cities' scattered about the region. The Thunder Rocks (and all the 'rock cities') are actually a layer of erosion-resistant rock which, over time, split apart and now appear to be completely separate huge boulders. The Thunder Rocks area is quite popular, so visit early in the morning for peace and quiet.

Red House and Quaker Lakes

These lakes are the center for many activities in the park. Most of the camping and cabin sights are close to the lakes.

Big Basin / Big Tree Old Growth Forest

This area contains one of several, but by far the largest, old growth forest areas within the boundaries of Allegany State Park. It may even be the largest old growth forest remnant in Western New York. Accounts differ on how much old growth forest is here, but it is generally agreed that there are 500 or more acres. In any case, it is a large area of old growth forest (probably the largest in this region north of the Pennsylvania border.).

Art Roscoe Ski Touring Area

18 miles of trails very popular with cross country skiers. The trails are wider and less hilly than others in the park, making them ideal for cross country skiing. Although these trails are tamer, the scenery is just as breathtaking.

Activities

Hiking, picnicking, camping, ball-playing, swimming, bicycling, nature appreciation, photography, and cross-country skiing and snowshoeing in the winter.

Amenities

Campgrounds and cabins, camp stores, a restaurant and bathhouses. Salamanca and the surrounding area have a wide range of accommodations.

Special Note

It is my belief that as more people become aware of the special places mentioned in this book, they will become more vigilant about protecting them. All of us who care about the integrity of these special places need to keep a constant vigil out for those who would destroy our parks and forests for financial gain. Can you imagine sharing your parks with buzzing chainsaws and diesel-belching logging trucks?

Recently, these interests attempted to open up Allegany to logging and natural resource exploitation under the guise of a 'management plan'. It is my contention that to do this would destroy the integrity of the park and the reason it was set aside in the first place. There are some things of value that you cannot put a price tag on and one of those is protecting, at almost any cost, the few sanctuaries left where Mother Nature is left to her own devices.

Allegany is our park and the great majority of New York State residents have made it clear they want 'hands-off' our parks. The issue of exploiting 'protected areas' like our parks is far from over. I have been informed that as this book went to press, bills were being introduced in Albany to exploit the natural resources of our parks statewide. Please join me in doing whatever you can to protect these significant pieces of our heritage!

Directions

From downtown Buffalo, access the Niagara Section of the NYS Thruway (Route 190) headed south. After about five miles, pick up the mainline NYS Thruway (Route 90) heading west. After another couple of miles, pick up Route 219 South. Follow Route 219 until the expressway section of it ends at Springville. Turn left, then right and continue on the surface section of Route 219 for about 28 miles to Salamanca. Turn right on Route 417 and follow the signs to Route 17 and head west. The Red House exit is about 6 miles from the entrance to Route 17. About 4 miles after the Red House exit is the Quaker Lake exit.

For directions to the 'special spots', visit the administration building. The administration building is located on Red House Lake. To find the administration building, enter the park via the Red House entrance and follow that road about two miles until you see the sign.

Eerie, misty morning on Quaker Lake.

Buttermilk Falls of Ithaca

QuikFinder™

Distance	160 miles
Direction	ESE
Nearest City/Town	Ithaca
Drivetime	3.5 hours

The Finger Lakes region was invaded by immense glaciers from the north during the last ice age. These glaciers excavated deep troughs in ancient river valleys. The sides of these valleys were shorn off and the valleys were deepened by the ice. As the glaciers receded and melted (the last one only about 10,000 years ago), the melt water eroded deep gorges into the sheer walls forming waterfalls and cascades and filling the Finger Lakes.

Pinnacle Rock towers over one of the many waterfalls along the Gorge Trail in Buttermilk State Park.

In Buttermilk Falls State Park, the erosion has left multiple waterfalls, towering cliffs, sculptured pools and a rock sculpture named Pinnacle Rock.

Another notable feature of the park is Lake Treman. The dam that impounds Lake Treman was built for a gristmill in 1875.

First Impression

As I hiked the trail along the creek for the first time I was quite in awe, as each time I crested a ridge or turned a corner on the Gorge Trail, a new set of natural marvels appeared before me. From the descriptions I had read I expected a pretty set of waterfalls and some nice gorge scenery. What I had not expected was the sheer number of scenic delights, one after another, non-stop along the entire trail.

Special Spot

The Gorge Trail along the side of the creek inside the gorge is glorious, especially when hiked off season or early in the morning when there are few other hikers. Every hundred feet or so there are new scenic delights - waterfalls, sluices, sculpted pools and natural rock sculptures.

Activities

Hiking, picnicking, camping, ball-playing, nature appreciation, photography, and cross-country skiing and snowshoeing in the winter.

The park has four trails:

Gorge Trail

Approximately 1 mile - the gorge trail follows the creek through the gorge and is a must hike trail. This trail allows you to get up close and intimate with the features that make this park special. Note: although the park is open year-round, the gorge trail is closed during the winter due to hazardous conditions.

Rim Trail

About 1 mile - follows the upper rim of the gorge. There are several overlooks along this trail giving a good perspective of how deep the gorge is.

Treman Lake Trail

About 2 miles - as you might have guessed, this trail follows the shoreline of the lake.

Nature Trail - Larch Meadow

Approximately 2 miles - this trail features a marshy area surviving from glacial times and is home to many interesting plant and animal species, some unique to these conditions and not found elsewhere.

Trail maps are available from the attendant in the booth at the park entrance. If the entrance booth is closed, the map is posted on the information board.

And, what visit to the Finger Lakes region would be complete without a wine tasting tour! There are well over 50 wineries in the region each with their own unique wines.

Amenities

Campgrounds, concession stand, restrooms on site. Nearby Ithaca and the surrounding area have a wide range of accommodations.

There are several other State Parks nearby (two are featured in this book - Watkins Glen and Taughannock Falls) with equally spectacular scenery.

Directions

From downtown Buffalo, access the Niagara Section of the NYS Thruway (Route 190) headed south. After about five miles, pick up the mainline NYS Thruway (Route 90) heading east. Stay on Route 90 for approximately 100 miles to exit 42. Take Route 14 south to Route 96 East (less than a mile). Follow Route 96 for about 50 miles into Ithaca. Turn right onto Route 13 South. Buttermilk Falls State Park is about two miles from the turn on the left hand side.

Chimney Bluffs

This undeveloped State Park contains a bizarre and amazing collection of eroded spires, pinnacles and ridges looking much like some of the incredible rock formations found out west. It is located along the Lake Ontario shoreline and stretches for about one half of a mile. As far as I know, there is nothing else remotely like it anywhere near Western New York.

QuikFinder™

Distance	140 miles
Direction	ENE
Nearest City/Town	Wolcott
Drivetime	2-1/2 - 3 hours

CANADA

ERIE

ONTARIO

BUFFALO

PENNSYLVANIA

A jagged peak points to the moon.

The amazing sculpting power of water and weather demonstrated at Chimney Bluffs.

Savoring the sunset across Lake Ontario from atop the bluffs.

First Impression

I couldn't believe what I was seeing! The views of the formations seen from both below and above are almost surreal. As you can see from the photos on the previous pages, it is hard to believe that the Chimney Bluffs are located in New York State. If the rocks were red and Lake Ontario was not right next to you, you would think you were somewhere in the desert southwest. This place is a true scenic treasure. We can all be glad that someone had the foresight to preserve the area as an undeveloped State Park.

Special Spot

Sitting on the cliffs behind the Bluffs watching as an incredible Lake Ontario sunset baths the bizarre shapes below you in subdued yellows, oranges and reds.

Activities

Hiking, canoeing, nature appreciation, photography.

Amenities

None. There are campgrounds in the general vicinity.

Directions

From downtown Buffalo, access the Niagara Section of the NYS Thruway (Route 190) headed south. After about five miles, pick up the mainline NYS Thruway (Route 90) heading east. Stay on Route 90 for approximately 105 miles to exit 41. Exit heading north on Route 414. Follow Route 414 to where it crosses Route 104 (about 18 miles from the Thruway exit). Continue straight past Route 104 on what is now called Garner Rd. After about 5 miles, Garner Rd. ends at East Bay Rd. Turn left (do not go straight) on East Bay Rd. and follow it to Chimney Bluffs.

Kinzua / Allegheny National Forest - Overview

QuikFinder™

Distance	75 miles plus
Direction	S
Nearest City/Town	Salamanca
Drivetime	2 hours plus

While many people are aware of the crown jewel of the New York State Park System - Allegany State Park, far fewer are aware of the unique treasures just across the NY/PA border in the Kinzua / Allegheny National Forest region. Yes, there is a difference in spelling - New York State uses 'Allegany' for the park and anything else named Allegany located in New York State, while the U.S. Forest Service and Pennsylvania use 'Allegheny' for the National Forest and anything named 'Allegheny' in Pennsylvania.

The Kinzua / Allegheny area is so large and has so much to offer I can only cover a small portion of what is available. I have chosen a few of my personal favorite areas, selected for proximity and scenic value:

• **The Allegheny Reservoir (91 miles of shoreline!)**

• **Scenic overlook parks - Jakes Rocks and Rimrock**

• **Tionesta Scenic Area**

The Allegheny National Forest is just over the border in Pennsylvania yet so many from Western New York are completely unaware that a National Forest is so close! The recreational opportunities are virtually unlimited - something for everyone. There are dozens of campgrounds both in the Forest and on the Allegheny Reservoir shoreline, hundreds and hundreds of miles of trails, sparkling lakes, pristine rivers and streams, hills, mountains and wildlife galore!

Much more information about this extensive area is available by stopping at the Visitor's Centers located throughout the region or by writing or calling:

The U.S. Forest Service
222 Liberty St., PO Box 847
Warren, PA 16365

1-814-723-5150

An Allegheny Mountain stream painted blue by the sky above.

Kinzua / Allegheny National Forest - Allegheny Reservoir

The Allegheny Reservoir was created in 1965 in the Allegheny River Valley by the construction of the Kinzua Dam. The purpose of the Dam is flood control but with that came new recreational and scenic opportunities. The Reservoir is 24 miles long in varying widths and has 91 miles of shoreline.

QuikFinder™

Distance	75 miles plus
Direction	S
Nearest City/Town	Salamanca
Drivetime	2 hours plus

A Great Blue Heron surveys Willow Bay for a meal.

The area is noted for the beautiful U.S. Forest Service campgrounds in the area (a total of ten) and the scenic overlook parks (see Overlooks - Jakes Rocks and Rimrock) offering fantastic views of the reservoir.

First Impression

I was surprised at how large and scenic the reservoir was. The Allegheny Reservoir is roughly comparable in size to the much better known (and much more developed) Chautauqua Lake. The reservoir is surrounded by lush forests and the rugged Allegheny Mountains and is a well kept secret among local nature enthusiasts and sportspeople.

Special Spot

The drive along New York Route 280 and Pennsylvania's Routes 346, 321 and 59 paralleling the reservoir is very scenic. It alternates between beautiful views of the reservoir, the mountains and the forests.

Activities

Swimming, canoeing, camping, hiking, nature appreciation, photography, and, in the winter, snowshoeing and cross-country skiing. The complete list of activities allowed in the area is quite extensive and is dependent on the season. Check with the U.S. Forest Service (address and phone number in the Overview) for a complete list of trails, allowable activities, facilities and other information.

Amenities

There are public (U.S. Forest Service) and private campgrounds in the area with varying facilities. There are also motels, hotels and bed and breakfasts scattered throughout the area.

Directions

From downtown Buffalo, access the Niagara Section of the NYS Thruway (Route 190) heading south. After about five miles, pick up the mainline NYS Thruway (Route 90) heading west. After another couple of miles pick up Route 219 South. Follow Route 219 until the expressway section of it ends at Springville. Turn left, then right and continue on the surface section of Route 219 for about 28 miles to Salamanca. Turn right on Route 417 and follow the signs to Route 17 West. Drive on Route 17 west for 11 miles and exit at NY Route 280 (also the exit for Allegany State Park - Quaker Lake Area). Follow Route 280 south (when you enter Pennsylvania it changes to Route 346). After about 10 miles on Routes 280/346 turn right on Route 321 South. To continue paralleling the Reservoir, make a right when you reach Route 59. After about ten miles, you will see the Kinzua Dam on your right hand side.

Kinzua / Allegheny National Forest - Scenic Overlooks: Jakes Rocks, Rimrock

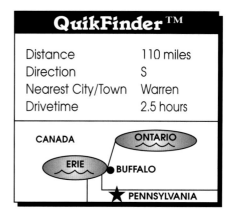

QuikFinder™

Distance	110 miles
Direction	S
Nearest City/Town	Warren
Drivetime	2.5 hours

Both Jakes Rocks and Rimrock are day use only parks in the Allegheny National Forest. They both offer spectacular views of the Allegheny Reservoir, the Allegheny Mountains, the Kinzua Dam and are also home to some very interesting rock formations.

The rock formations are similar to those found at Little Rock City (included in this book) and in many other 'rock cities' scattered about the countryside of Western New York and Northwestern Pennsylvania. All the 'rock cities' are actually a layer of erosion-resistant rock which, over time, split apart and now appears to be completely separate huge boulders.

First Impression

The Views - The lush and lavish scenery of the Kinzua area is certainly notable at ground level, but when I saw the area for the first time from the vantage point of the overlooks it took on a whole new perspective - simply breathtaking.

The reservoir gently winding off into the distance following the old river valley reminded me of the lush river valleys of the Northwest. The soft forests blanketing the hills reach down and touch the waters edge as far as the eye can see, giving the illusion of untouched wilderness - a most refreshing sight.

The Rocks - Massive. Monstrous. Mind-boggling. Walking the trails below the boulders and cliffs, these rocks tower above and are almost overwhelming. The long, steep, narrow stone stairway that snakes down between boulders at Rimrock has a distinctly medieval feel to it. The cracks, crevices and caves could conceivably have once been home to bears or ancient peoples.

Special Spot

At Rimrock, the view of the Reservoir from the overlooks is simply stunning. The reservoir appears endless as it melts into the hills to the north. The sight of the multitude of quiet coves along the shoreline is balm for the stressed out mind as one easily pictures the peace and solitude inside the sheltered bays.

Indian Cave at Jakes Rocks is fascinating. The sheer immensity of the giant rockslab looming overhead with no visible means of support is daunting. It seems a likely spot to find Indian cave drawings or petroglyphs although I was unable to find any evidence of Indian habitation.

Giant boulders loom eerily in the mist along the Rimrock base trail.

Activities

Hiking, picnicking, nature appreciation, photography, view-bagging and, in the winter, cross-country skiing and snowshoeing. I suggest you also visit the Kinzua Dam while in the area. It is quite a feat of engineering.

Right - The stone staircase at Rimrock has a magical, medieval feel to it.

The lush forests and placid waters make this a scene you won't soon forget.

Both Rimrock and Jakes Rocks have trails to the scenic overlooks and trails along the base of the rocks and cliffs. The Morrison Hiking Trail which includes the Rimrock Trail Loop passes through the Rimrock area. Look for off-white diamond trail markers.

Amenities

Restrooms, picnic tables and grills, drinking water.

Directions

From downtown Buffalo, access the Niagara Section of the NYS Thruway (Route 190) heading south. After about 5 miles, pick up the mainline NYS Thruway (Route 90) heading west. After another couple of miles pick up Route 219 South. Follow Route 219 until the expressway section of it ends at Springville. Turn left, then right and continue on the surface section of Route 219 for about 28 miles to Salamanca. Turn right on Route 417 and follow the signs to Route 17 West. Drive on Route 17 west for 11 miles and exit at NY Route 280 (also the exit for Allegany State Park - Quaker Lake Area). Follow Route 280 South (when you enter Pennsylvania it changes to Route 346). After about 10 miles on Routes 280/346 turn right on Route 321 South. You have been paralleling the reservoir. Follow Route 321 south to Route 59. Turn right (west).

Rimrock is on the left off Route 59 about 7 miles from the turn from Route 321 onto Route 59 (look for the sign).

For ***Jakes Rocks*** continue past Rimrock about 3 miles. Immediately after crossing the bridge over an arm of the reservoir, turn left on Route 262 (look for the Jakes Rocks sign). Follow Route 262 up the hill for a little over a mile and you will see the Jakes Rocks turnoff to the right (look for the sign). Follow this road until you see the signs for parking and the scenic overlooks.

To see the ***Kinzua Dam,*** continue on Route 59 past the turnoff for Jakes Rocks. Parking for the Dam is about a mile past the turnoff on your right.

For an added treat, look for a small dirt parking area on your left hand side, just before the Kinzua Dam. To your right as you pull into the parking area is a picturesque boulder-strewn stream with a pretty set of waterfalls.

Kinzua / Allegheny National Forest - Tionesta Scenic Area

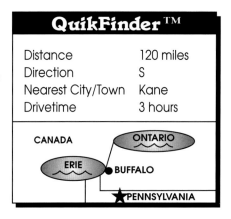

QuikFinder ™

Distance	120 miles
Direction	S
Nearest City/Town	Kane
Drivetime	3 hours

An area of sharp contrasts - you can compare the beauty and spirit of old growth forest to two different types of devastation - clear-cut logging and tornadoes. The sign describing the area states that there are more than 2,000 acres of old growth forest here. Between logging and tornado devastation, much less remains.

First Impression

What happened here? At first I thought that once again, logging interests had nearly destroyed the entire area. I later found out that a tornado had cut a swath through the forest and that some of the logging was due to a salvage operation after the tornado.

Special Spot

Walk the old growth trail, stand at the base of a 400 year old tree and look up. Try to imagine all that has occurred while this tree has been alive. After feeling the spirit of the old growth, compare that feeling to the feeling you get in the tornado swath and clear-cut areas. Resolve to help save the last of the old growth forests in our country.

Activities

Hiking, nature appreciation, photography.

There are two trails here:

The *Tionesta Scenic Area Interpretive Trail* is a loop trail about 1 mile in length and is marked with grey blazes.

The *North Country National Scenic Trail (NCNST)* traverses the Tionesta Scenic Area and sports blue blazes.

For those who enjoy hiking, I recommend hiking the NCNST south for several miles. You will be rewarded by seeing the tornado swath, a 'rock city', the south branch of Tionesta Creek in addition to the Scenic Area itself.

Amenities

None.

Directions

From downtown Buffalo, access the Niagara Section of the NYS Thruway (Route 190) heading south. After about 5 miles, pick up the mainline NYS Thruway (Route 90) heading west. After another couple of miles pick up Route 219 South. Follow Route 219 until the expressway section of it ends at Springville. Turn left, then right and continue on the surface section of Route 219 for about 28 miles to Salamanca. Turn right on Route 417 and follow the signs to Route 17 West. Drive on Route 17 west for 11 miles and exit at NY Route 280 (also the exit for Allegany State Park - Quaker Lake Area). Follow Route 280 south (when you enter Pennsylvania it changes to Route 346). After about 10 miles on Routes 280/346 turn right on Route 321 South. You have been paralleling the reservoir. Follow Route 321 south to Route 59.

See and feel the magic of a towering 400 year old tree in the Tionesta Scenic Area.

Turn right (west). Proceed about two miles on Route 59 and turn left, again picking up Route 321 South. Proceed on Route 321 about 10 miles to Gibbs Hill Rd. and turn right. Drive about 4 miles on Gibbs Hill until it ends at Route 6. Turn right. Within the next mile or so look on your left for Forest Road 133 (FS 133). Turn left onto FS 133. Follow the signs sprinkled along FS 133 to the Tionesta Scenic area. These directions can be difficult to follow - bring a good map.

Taughannock Falls State Park

The Finger Lakes region was invaded during the last ice age by immense glaciers from the north. These glaciers excavated deep troughs in ancient river valleys. The sides of these valleys were shorn off and the valleys were deepened by the ice. As the glaciers receded and melted (the last one only about 10,000 years ago), the melt water eroded deep gorges into the sheer walls forming waterfalls and cascades and filled the Finger Lakes.

QuikFinder™

Distance	150 miles
Direction	ESE
Nearest City/Town	Trumansburg
Drivetime	3 hours

At 215 feet, Taughannock falls further than Niagara!

Beyond Buffalo!

There are several interpretations of the Indian word "Taughannock". One interpretation is that it means "Great Fall in the Woods". Indeed, Taughannock is 215 feet high, higher than Niagara Falls! It is the highest straight drop waterfall in the Northeastern United States. The walls on either side of the falls are nearly 400 feet high.

When the glaciers receded after the last ice age, Taughannock Falls fell directly into Cayuga Lake. Over 10,000 years, erosion has dug into the hillside increasing their height and moving the falls back 3/4 of a mile from the original location!

Here is how the waterfalls work: the rock at the top of the falls is limestone which is much harder than the shale below it. The stream erodes the shale below more quickly and easily leaving an exposed layer of limestone from which the water tumbles. In time, with no support below, the limestone ledge breaks off and the process continues.

The shale breaks down and gets washed toward the lake by the creek. The shale is then deposited into the lake and over the years has formed a delta called Taughannock Point. Including Taughannock Point, the park has one mile of shoreline.

First Impression

What can I say about my first impression of seeing a waterfall higher than Niagara Falls? Awesome! And somehow, just knowing that this waterfall will continue its persistant march into the hillside further increasing its height, adds to the thrill.

Hiking in to the falls, the closer I got to the base the more impressed I was. Viewing the falls from the top overlook, the falls are impressive, but hearing and feeling the effect of water falling 215 feet and crashing into the plunge pool has a profound effect.

I tried to imagine the time when the first settlers of the region discovered the falls - they must have been awestruck! There were other falls in the area, but none with a straight drop of this magnitude. In fact, our forefathers were so impressed that in the 1800's, they built two hotels here - one on each side of the gorge overlooking the falls!

Special Spot

At the end of the trail, near the base of the falls. By getting that close and being doused by mist, you will be amazed what power modest amounts of water descending great distances can have. The falls are especially wondrous during spring melt or after a heavy rain when the volume is greatly increased.

Activities

Hiking, picnicking, camping, ball-playing, nature appreciation, photography, and, during the winter, tobogganing, sledding, beginner downhill skiing, cross-country skiing, snowshoeing and ice skating.

The park has two trails:

Gorge Trail - Approximately 1 and 1/2 miles roundtrip - the gorge trail follows the creek upstream to the base of the falls and is relatively level and flat - accessible to almost everyone.

Rim Trail - About 3/4 mile - follows the upper rim of the gorge from the upper overlook to the bottom parking area.

This is Finger Lakes Wine Country. Take a wine tasting tour! There are well over 50 unique wineries in the region.

Amenities

Campgrounds, cabins, a concession stand, picnic tables with firepits, restrooms on site. The park has a warm-up shelter for winter activities. Ithaca, about 15 miles away, and the surrounding area, offer a wide range of accommodations. There are several other State Parks nearby (including two featured in this book - Watkins Glen and Buttermilk Falls) with more spectacular scenery.

Directions

From downtown Buffalo, access the Niagara Section of the NYS Thruway (Route 190) heading south. After about 5 miles, pick up the mainline NYS Thruway (Route 90) heading east. Stay on Route 90 for approximately 100 miles to exit 42. Take Route 14 south to Route 96 east (less than a mile). Follow Route 96 for about 30 miles to Route 96A. Turn left. Drive about 1 mile and turn right on Route 89. After about 7 miles, you will see signs for the park. Follow the signs into the park.

Taughannock Falls framed in fall colors.

Watkins Glen

The Finger Lakes region was invaded during the last ice age by immense glaciers from the north. These glaciers excavated deep troughs in ancient river valleys. The sides of these valleys were shorn off and the valleys were deepened by the ice. As the glaciers receded and melted (the last one only about 10,000 years ago), the melt water eroded deep gorges into the sheer walls forming waterfalls and cascades and filled the Finger Lakes.

QuikFinder™

Distance	150 miles
Direction	ESE
Nearest City/Town	Watkins Glen
Drivetime	3 hours

Watkins Glen is a treasure trove of scenic delights!

Watkins Glen was originally a privately owned and operated tourist resort. It was founded in 1863. Since then many have marveled at the beauty created by the incredible sculpting power of water. There are a total of 19 waterfalls in all shapes and forms including a couple you can walk behind. Other interesting features include 'plunge pools', 'pot holes' and a wide variety of sculpted rock formations.

Of all the entries in this book, Watkins Glen may be among the best known. However, many people I have spoken to, though aware of it, have not been there. I have included it to urge those who have not visited the Glen to do it - it is a 'must see' wonderland kind of place, called by some "The Eighth Wonder of the World".

First Impression

I must be dreaming, this place cannot be real! It is real. As mentioned above, it has a storybook or wonderland feel to it. I could see why some call Watkins Glen "The Eighth Wonder of the World". If you have not seen it yet, go - you will be amazed!

Special Spot

The entire Glen is a series of scenic delights - it is impossible to pick one 'special spot'. A few of the highlights include two different waterfalls you can walk behind, ruggedly beautiful stone bridges and walkways, hand-cut tunnels in the rock and a suspension bridge dangling 85 feet above the gorge.

Activities

Hiking, picnicking, camping, swimming (in a pool, not in the gorge itself), ball playing, nature appreciation, photography, and, in the winter, cross-country skiing and snowshoeing.

Guided walks are led by park staff at scheduled times.

A sound and light show called "Timespell" illustrates the story of Watkins Glen twice an evening from May through October. There is a separate admission charge for the show.

The park has three trails, all linking the Upper and Main entrances and each about 1.5 miles one way. The gorge trails are closed in the winter due to hazardous conditions.

Gorge Trail

Follows Glen Creek through the gorge and is the most scenic trail. The trail is steep and slippery in places.

South Rim Trail

Winds along the south rim of the gorge providing several overlooks into the gorge.

Indian Trail

Meanders along the north rim with some stunning aerial views of the gorge.

Amenities

Campgrounds, concession stand, restrooms on site. The Village of Watkins Glen and surrounding area has a wide range of accommodations and facilities.

There are several other State Parks nearby (two are featured in this book - Buttermilk Falls and Taughannock Falls) with similar spectacular scenery.

And, what visit to the Finger Lakes region would be complete without a wine tasting tour! There are well over 50 wineries in the region each with their own unique wines.

Directions

From downtown Buffalo, access the Niagara Section of the NYS Thruway (Route 190) heading south. After about 5 miles, pick up the mainline NYS Thruway (Route 90) heading east. Stay on Route 90 for approximately 100 miles to exit 42. Take Route 14 south about 45 miles into the Village of Watkins Glen. The main entrance to the park is on the right at the far end of the village.

Weekenders

Inman Gulf

Spectacular gorge scenery without the crowds! Inman Gulf is one of the unique Tug Hill Plateau gorges carved out by many years of stream erosion. Inman Gulf is located on New York State land and has excellent, well maintained trails thanks to some very dedicated volunteers. The trails have great views into the gorge and of several waterfalls.

QuikFinder™

Distance	210 miles
Direction	ENE
Nearest City/Town	Watertown
Drivetime	4 hours

CANADA
ONTARIO
ERIE
BUFFALO
PENNSYLVANIA

First Impression

Great views, wonderful trails and few visitors! If you enjoy gorge scenery but prefer to be away from blacktop and crowds, you will love the Inman Gulf trails. I never imagined the trails would be as nice as they are - very scenic, natural and very well maintained.

Special Spot

The incredible view of Rainbow Falls from the Inman Gulf Glide trail. This waterfall is beautifully shaped - it's picture perfect! Visit this special spot in the late spring when the water is really flowing, or in winter when the falls become a large frozen ice sculpture.

Picture perfect Rainbow Falls as seen from the Inman Gulf Glide Trail.

Activities

Hiking, nature appreciation, photography, and, in the winter, snowshoeing and cross-country skiing.

There are three maintained trails:

Oak Rim Trail

2.45 miles - this trail features two benches at dramatic view points, some huge old oaks and sweeping vistas of the gulf. This trail is not suitable for cross-country skiing due to its proximity to the edge in many places.

John Young Trail

.98 miles - this trail is wider and safer - great for cross-country skiing. There is a picnic area along the trail.

Inman Gulf Glide

1.48 miles - as mentioned above, the view of Rainbow Falls is the crowning glory of this trail. The trail has some ups and downs and should be skied only by experienced cross-country skiers.

Amenities

None. There are campgrounds in the area and camping is allowed on State Land. The nearest town with accommodations and facilities is Watertown (about 20 miles away).

Directions

From downtown Buffalo, access the Niagara Section of the NYS Thruway (Route 190) headed south. After about five miles, pick up the mainline NYS Thruway (Route 90) heading east. Stay on Route 90 for approximately 155 miles to Route 81 North. Take Route 81 north about 55 miles to exit 42. Exit heading east on Route 177. Follow Route 177 to Williams Road (about 8 miles). Williams Road is on the left and just before the road you will see a large sign announcing the Tug Hill State Forest. The first trailhead and parking area is on your right only several hundred yards from the turn onto Williams Road. The other trailheads are also on the right hand side of Williams Road (look for the corresponding parking areas).

Killarney Wilderness Park

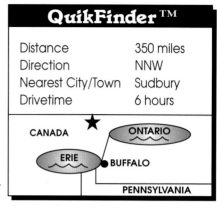

QuikFinder™

Distance	350 miles
Direction	NNW
Nearest City/Town	Sudbury
Drivetime	6 hours

Killarney is so many things I almost don't know where to start. Killarney is pink granite lakeshores and ancient mountains of white quartz. Killarney is crystal-clear, deep blue lakes and steep walled fiords. Killarney is emerald green forests and meadows of white birch. Killarney is picture-postcard vistas and unbroken wilderness. Killarney is the late night howl of timber wolves and the eerie dawn call of the loon.

Killarney is an Ontario Provincial Park and until recently, almost unknown. Recent years have seen the building of a visitors center and sharply increased visitation, but despite all that, it is still a jewel to behold.

Billions of years ago a huge mountain system higher and more extensive than the Rockies lay to the north of Killarney. The erosion of these mountains funneled into the adjoining areas, and in time, these sediments hardened into rock. Later, the land under these sediments rose forming the La Cloche Mountains of which a mere stubble remains today in the northern 75% of the park.

Years later, another mountain building episode took place, this time in the southern section of the park. These mountains gave rise to granitic igneous rock, or Killarney Pink Granite. In succeeding years, in the extreme southeastern portion of the park, Glenville rocks were twisted, folded and fractured by extreme pressures and temperatures and now dominate.

After these major events, glaciation took place at least four times over the last million years, rounding and shaping the landscape. The building of Killarney as we see it today took over 3.5 billion years.

First Impression

In preparation for my first trip to Killarney I read what others had written about the park. They all told of a very beautiful place. Their descriptions of white quartz mountains, pink granite lake shores and crystal clear lake waters sounded wonderful. Of the 6 hour drive from Buffalo, the last 3 hours were quite scenic - lakes, forests, glimpses of the Georgian Bay - beautiful 'cottage country' (as the Canadians call it) scenery. As I approached the park, I expected Killarney to be similar. Even though the descriptions I had read mentioned the La Cloche Mountains, I hadn't seen anything even resembling a mountain so I assumed the 'mountains' were just forested hills.

Beyond Buffalo!

I entered the park and stopped at the self-service pay station to pay for my site. I proceeded into the campground and got my first glimpse across Lake George and *Whoa!* - there they were, the gleaming white mountains, plunging into a deep blue jewel of a lake trimmed in pink granite. I was stunned! The scenery was better than beautiful (if that is possible). This was one of those rare times in life when I expected the best and my expectations were exceeded, and by a significant amount!

The breathtaking views from atop the La Cloche Mountains of Killarney.

To get an impression of how others felt about Killarney, I spoke with some of the locals during my numerous trips there. They all felt they lived in a very special, almost mystical place. One couple told me they had traveled the world trying to decide where to settle down when they happened to stumble on Killarney and immediately decided Killarney was it. Does that tell you something about the wonder of this place?

Right: Chikanishing Creek winds off toward the Georgian Bay.

A quiet Killarney cove.

Beyond Buffalo!

Special Spot

Picking out just one 'special spot' in Killarney is not possible. Everywhere you go here is incredibly scenic. But if forced to pick just one spot, I would have to pick the view from Killarney Ridge deep in the La Cloche Mountains. On a clear day you can see far out into the Georgian Bay and, in all other directions, countless miles of gleaming white mountains, azure lakes, and soft evergreen forest.

Fortunately, since this is my book and I do not have to pick just one spot, I have included two other spots as well:

First, the beautiful wave-washed point protruding into the Georgian Bay at the end of the Chikanishing Trail. Here you have gorgeous views of the Bay and a few small islands, and the lunar landscape of the weather-beaten rocks of the Precambrian Shield.

The other spot is any campsite along the cliff overlooking George Lake in the eastern portion of the campground. Long ago I once said that these campsites were the most beautiful sites in the world. I haven't changed my mind since! The view of the nearby pink granite reflected in the lake waters, the white quartzite mountains shining in the distance and the deep blue water shimmering in the sunlight is stunning. And waking to the eerie, reverberating call of the loons echoing down the lake makes for an unforgettable experience.

Activities

Hiking, camping, interior camping, canoeing, picnicking, nature appreciation, photography, and, in the winter, cross-country skiing and snowshoeing.

There are 5 hiking trails in the area that I am aware of (and I am sure there are more). For details, pick up information at the visitors center:

Cranberry Bog - 2.5 miles - picturesque landscapes, gorgeous views of A.Y. Jackson Lake nestled among pink granite cliffs, bogs, marshes and swamps. Plentiful wildlife and wetland plant life.

LaCloche Silhouette - 63 miles in entirety but two sections can be done as dayhikes. I suggest the following:

The Baie Fine Section - about 9 miles roundtrip to the waterfalls of Artist Creek which flows between Artist Lake and Baie Fine. This section of trail passes by numerous beaver dams, groves of white birch, picturesque brooks, a couple of remnant 'old growth' tree stands and numerous views of the mountains. There is a side trail to Lumsden Lake.

The East Section - about 13 miles roundtrip to the incredible vistas from Killarney Ridge. This is a strenuous and lengthy trip for a day hike. I recommend canoeing to the base of the ridge and then hiking to the top. However, in order to canoe to the base, you should be an experienced canoeist - there are two portages and the winds on the open lakes can be tricky. Speak with park personnel for more information on the route.

Chikanishing - 2 mile loop. This trail was described in the 'special spot' section. The trail starts at the end of Chikanishing Road. The last time I visited, the road was washed out in spots and looked more like a four wheel drive trail.

Granite Ridge - Just over a mile. Offers 2 scenic vistas of the Georgian Bay area to the south and the mountain ridges to the north.

East Lighthouse/Tar Vat Bay - 3 mile loop. This hike parallels the Georgian Bay. It gets its name from a small bay where fisherman tarred their nets to protect them.

For canoeists, there is an almost endless variety of canoe routes depending on how experienced you are, how many portages you are willing to make and how long you wish to canoe.

Amenities

The park has both campground camping and interior camping. The campground camping is primitive - pit toilets and no electricity, but does have running water. The nearby town of Killarney has accommodations and a variety of facilities.

Directions

From downtown Buffalo, access the Niagara Section of the NYS Thruway (Route 190) heading North. Follow the signs to the Peace Bridge and enter Canada. As you proceed from the customs area, take the Queen Elizabeth Way (QEW) north. Take the QEW approximately 90 miles to Route 427 North (just before Toronto). After 5 miles, exit to Route 401 East. In about 4 miles, exit onto Route 400 North. Take Route 400 for about 80 miles to where it ends and becomes Route 69. Continue on Route 69 for approximately 135 miles and then turn left on Route 637. Follow Route 637 to the Park entrance on the right (about 35 miles).

Pine Creek Gorge - The Grand Canyon of PA

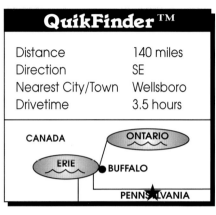

QuikFinder™

Distance	140 miles
Direction	SE
Nearest City/Town	Wellsboro
Drivetime	3.5 hours

CANADA — ONTARIO — ERIE — BUFFALO — PENNSYLVANIA

The Pine Creek Gorge is a lush, dramatic, glacial runoff carved canyon located in north-central Pennsylvania. The canyon is over 800 feet deep in places and extends for 47 miles. A 12 mile section of the gorge is a National Natural Landmark as designated by the U.S. National Park Service. The northern most section of the gorge runs through the Tioga State Forest.

The story behind the gorge: from about 1.8 million years ago until just 10,000 years ago, glaciers covered the area just north of the canyon. The canyon was formed when glaciation blocked the creek, which originally ran north-easterly, and caused it to be diverted into what is now known as the 'Grand Canyon of PA'.

First Impression

We in the Buffalo area often don't know enough about our neighboring state to the south. Here is a magnificent gorge, dubbed the 'Grand Canyon of Pennsylvania' and neither I nor anyone I knew had heard of it.

Pine Creek Gorge - The 'Grand Canyon of Pennsylvania'

A mere three hours from the City of Buffalo and unknown to most of us!

As I drove along Route 6 the first time I visited Pine Creek, I had a hard time believing that the gentle, but good sized creek flowing next to me was the same one that plunges through the canyon. Seeing the canyon for the first time was impressive in part because there are so many accessible scenic views - dozens if not hundreds of vistas from which it can be observed.

Activities

The Canyon region encompasses such a large area that just about any activity that you can imagine is possible at some time of the year somewhere in the canyon area. There are several campgrounds and picnic areas, dozens of hiking and biking trails, outfitters for canoeing and kayaking, stables for horseback riding and much more.

Along Four Mile Run, water spills over protruding ledges on its way to meet Pine Creek.

Beyond Buffalo!

The west side of the canyon is the more commercialized of the two sides with a privately owned zoo, a small airport providing canyon overflights and private campgrounds. The east side (which I much prefer) is in a much more natural state and is almost exclusively in the Tioga State Forest. Each side features a Pennsylvania State Park showcasing spectacular views.

For more information about hikes in the Grand Canyon area, I recommend "Short Hikes in Pennsylvania's Grand Canyon" by Chuck Dillon, published by Pine Creek Press. Pine Creek Press also has several other Canyon related publications available:

Pine Creek Press

R.R. 4 Box 130B

Wellsboro, PA 16901

717-724-3003

Amenities

Most amenities are available in the Canyon area. Specific amenities include campgrounds, Bed & Breakfasts, restaurants, outfitters and picnic areas.

Directions

From downtown Buffalo, access the Niagara Section of the NYS Thruway (Route 190) heading south. After about five miles, pick up the mainline NYS Thruway (Route 90) heading west. About a mile later, exit onto Route 400 South. Stay on Route 400 until it ends (about 15 miles) and becomes Route 16. Continue on Route 16 for roughly 12 miles to Route 39 East. Turn left on Route 39 East and drive through the Village of Arcade to Route 98 South. Follow Route 98 South about 8 miles to Route 243 South (no turn required, just continue straight as Route 98 turns right). Take Route 243 about ten miles to where it ends at Route 19. Turn right on Route 19 heading south through the towns of Belfast, Belmont and Wellsville to the Pennsylvania state line. The Route number changes to 449 as you enter PA. Continue on Route 449 from the state line about 15 more miles to Route 6. Turn left heading east on Route 6. After about 20 miles you will see signs directing you to the Grand Canyon area. The west side of the Canyon is accessed off State Forest roads (look for the sign) and the east side is accessed off Route 362 (also indicated by signs).

Stillwater / Beaver River

QuikFinder ™

Distance	240 miles
Direction	ENE
Nearest City/Town	Lowville
Drivetime	5 hours

The Stillwater Reservoir / Beaver River region encompasses some of the wildest country in the Northeast United States. The region is bounded by areas with names like Pepperbox Wilderness, Five Ponds Wilderness and Independence River Wild Forest. There is only one unimproved road through hundreds of square miles of wild beauty. In fact, the hamlet of Beaver River is unique in that it is only accessible by water.

The area is in the foothills of the Adirondacks and contains many ponds and lakes, rivers and streams, mountain summits and large unbroken tracts of forest.

First Impression

I got my first impression of the area when I was 10 years old - and I loved it. I stayed for a week at a camp in the area. This was my first taste of true wilderness and it succeeded in whetting my appetite for more.

Special Spot

The drive between the small towns of Number Four and Big Moose is one of the most remote and undeveloped public roads in New York State. You can feel the wilderness on all sides - so rare in this part of the country.

Because the Stillwater/Beaver River area contains relatively short mountains when compared to other parts of the Adirondacks, and because access to this area is more difficult, you won't encounter many other visitors here like you would in other areas. This helps add to the wilderness feel.

Activities

Hiking, camping, interior camping, canoeing, picnicking, nature appreciation, photography, and, in the winter, cross-country skiing and showshoeing.

The only designated trail in the Stillwater area that I am aware of is the Stillwater Mountain and Firetower Trail. This trail leads through majestic hardwoods to a firetower. From the firetower (if open), great vistas of the surrounding area can be seen. There are also old forest and logging roads that make acceptable hiking trails.

Amenities

None. The nearest accommodations are in Eagle Bay, about 20 miles south of

Morning Mist.

the Stillwater Reservoir by mainly unimproved road or back in Lowville. Primitive camping is allowed on the State Land in the vicinity.

Directions

From downtown Buffalo, access the Niagara Section of the NYS Thruway (Route 190) heading south. After about 5 miles, pick up the mainline NYS Thruway (Route 90) heading east. Stay on Route 90 for approximately 155 miles and exit onto Route 81 North. Take Route 81 north about 55 miles to exit 42. Exit heading east on Route 177. Follow Route 177 about 13 miles to Route 12. Take Route 12 south about 4 miles into Lowville where you pick up Route 812 North. Just outside of Lowville turn right on the Number Four Road. Follow Number Four Road to the hamlet of Number Four. Turn right on Stillwater - Big Moose Road. The Stillwater Reservoir is about 10 miles from Number Four. The Stillwater - Big Moose Road is unimproved and can be rough in places.

Whetstone Gulf State Park

Another of the unique Tug Hill Plateau gorges carved out by many years of stream erosion (also *see* Inman Gulf). This gorge is simply gorgeous. Whetstone features trails that follow both rims of the gorge from beginning to end with plenty of scenic vistas in between.

QuikFinder™

Distance	230 miles
Direction	ENE
Nearest City/Town	Lowville
Drivetime	4.5 hours

CANADA
ONTARIO
ERIE
BUFFALO
PENNSYLVANIA

Amid towering gorge walls, the waters of Whetstone ceaselessly dig deeper into the Tug Hill Plateau.

First Impression

The first time I visited Whetstone, I hiked the rim trails and was enchanted by the scenery - lots of gorge overlooks and several waterfalls cascading off the sides. Along the north trail, I spotted a raven's nest built in a notch on the opposite cliff wall. I decided to stop and watch. The nest was quiet but I could see several little heads poking out. After a couple of minutes, the mother came flying into view. The young, who knew they were about to be fed, began squeaking and squawking. The chorus increased the closer she came. Finally, they reached a soft crescendo with their immature little voices just as she landed on the nest with food in her mouth. I watched for a while as the young family went through the same routine over and over again - the mother would fly away searching for food and would be gone for about five minutes. The nestlings would become silent. As soon as the mother came into view returning with more food, the young would again begin their 'feed me' chorus, increasing with intensity as she approached.

Special Spot

The box canyon and waterfall at the end of the gorge-bottom trail. This hike is not for the faint of heart. Expect to get cold and wet. When I hiked this trail, it was the end of May and it was so cold in the canyon my fingers could barely operate the camera. At times, I was shivering intensely. There were still patches of snow along the canyon walls. I imagine in the heat of midsummer it would be a refreshing hike, yet still quite chilly as, quite literally, the sun never shines in parts of this canyon.

At the beginning of the hike, the chasm was about 100 feet wide. The stream, which was running quite full after several days of rain, meandered across the floor of the gorge. At first I was able to stay dry, but as the walls began closing in, there was no way to avoid getting wet. Soon the walls were only 15 to 20 feet apart. In order to keep making progress, I had to wade in and fight the currents which were intensifying as the water was funneled through smaller and smaller channels. The rushing sound of the water, intensified by the closeness of the canyon walls, combined with the feeling that the force of the water could knock me off my feet at any time was both thrilling and disconcerting. I was not worried about surviving, but I was worried about dousing my camera and equipment.

Next, I arrived at an eight foot crashing waterfall and thought that I would not be able to go on until I spotted a small area where the water was less intense and there were foot and hand holds. I fought through the current and climbed the falls. I was rewarded on the other side by a heavenly, sun-sparkled waterfall cascading down the steep north wall of the canyon. I then looked ahead - the canyon was narrowing to about 6 feet and, naturally, the water's power was intensified by that factor. I looked down to the other end of the box canyon and saw raging water, foam and flying mist. The explorer in me could not resist - I had to see what was causing the uproar at the other end.

I waded against the powerful current keeping my body sideways to slip through. The water was getting deeper and I was once again fearing for my equipment. I finally had to climb the last ten feet or so of the box canyon clinging to the rock wall - searching for hand and foot holds with frozen fingers and toes. One false move and both me and my equipment would be rushing back downstream out of control. Somehow, I made it to the end and was rewarded with a magnificent, thundering waterfall. The waterfall was about 15 feet high and was bursting through an opening of about six feet. All the waterpower of this rushing stream was squeezed into this small opening - the energy was intense. It was impossible to climb this waterfall - it was far too powerful and concentrated. This was the end of the hike, but what an ending!

Activities

Hiking, picnicking, swimming, camping, ball-playing, nature appreciation, photography, and, during the winter, cross-country skiing and snowshoeing.

Amenities

Whetstone Gulf is a campground with the usual campground amenities. The closest alternative accommodations and facilities are in Lowville, about 8 miles away.

Directions

From downtown Buffalo, access the Niagara Section of the NYS Thruway (Route 190) heading south. After about 5 miles, pick up the mainline NYS Thruway (Route 90) heading east. Stay on Route 90 for approximately 155 miles to Route 81 North. Take Route 81 north about 55 miles to exit 42. Exit heading east on Route 177. Follow Route 177 about 13 miles to Route 12. Take Route 12 south about 4 miles to Route 26 South. Whetstone is on the right hand side about 8 miles outside of Lowville.

Reflection and refraction impart chromatic delight to the waters of Whetstone.